JOURNEY TO ALLAH SERIES

WHO IS ALLAH?

A PRACTICAL GUIDE TO KNOWING ALLAH

FAITH Publications

All thanks are due to Allah *subhaanahu wa ta'ala* for enabling us with this effort.
Special thanks to the following contributors:

Content Writers: Umm Eesa and Dr. Haroon Baqai
Islamic Studies Curriculum Editing Team: Amber Bokhari, Br. Abdul Qaadir Abdul Khaaliq, Samira Hingoro
Graphic and Layout Design: Farah Firman

Copyright © 2024 FAITH Publications
3rd Edition

All rights reserved.
No part of this publication may be reproduced, distributed, or transmitted in any form or by any means, including photocopying, recording, or other electronic or mechanical methods, without the prior written permission of the publisher, except in the case of brief quotations embodied in critical reviews and certain other noncommercial uses permitted by copyright law.

Printed in the United States of America

ISBN 979-8-9874006-4-7

For permission requests, write to the publisher at the address below.

FAITH Publications
5301 Edgewood Road
College Park, MD 20740, USA
Phone: 301-982-9848
Email: info@faithpublications.org
Website: faithpublications.org

TABLE OF CONTENTS

UNIT 1 | WHO IS ALLAH?

CHAPTER	PG	
01	11	Knowing Allah
02	21	Allah is Merciful
03	33	Allah Answers Me
04	49	Allah Forgives Me
05	63	Allah Appreciates Me
06	71	Allah Loves Me
07	79	Allah is The Most High
08	85	Allah is One

UNIT 2 | WORSHIPING ALLAH

CHAPTER	PG	
09	93	Worshiping Allah Only
10	107	Living Between Hope & Fear
11	113	How Worship is Accepted?

PREFACE

We live in a rapidly changing world where conflicting views and opinions shape how we see the world and how we see ourselves. With information overload comes confusion and stress, especially for young people who are amid self-discovery. Young people like you.

Now more than ever, it is imperative for high school students to have complete certainty in Islam. Our belief system has been meticulously preserved for over fourteen centuries, and our faith has always proved its truth when challenged by every man-made ideology. A proper understanding of your faith will anchor you in today's world of doubts, disbelief, and self-centeredness.

This is the second book in the "Journey to Allah" series on Islamic belief that explores Allah's Oneness in His Names and Attributes (*Tawheed-ul-Asmaai was-Sifaat*) and Allah's Oneness in Worship (*Tawheed-ul-Uloohiyyah*). It provides answers to some frequently asked questions: Who is Allah? How does knowing Allah's Names and Attribute affect my life? Why should we worship Allah? What does submission to Allah look like? Should I follow what I think is right, or should I follow what Allah has asked me to do?

After having countless conversations with young people who asked these same questions, we wrote this book. We have seen what happens when they get answers. This book will help you begin your journey to know Allah, and that journey will transform the way you view and feel about yourself, others, and the world.

As part of a new, courageous Islamic Studies series, *'Who is Allah?'* aims to help you apply your faith to real-world issues. Features like the *Brain Teaser* boxes and the *Review and Reflect* sections show everyday, practical applications of our beliefs. We pray that this book helps you draw closer to Allah. We would love to improve this book with your suggestions. Please send your feedback to info@faithpublications.org.

Lastly, we would like to thank Umm Eesaa and Dr. Haroon Baqai for writing these units so beautifully. May Allah accept the effort of everyone who worked on this book, and more importantly, may Allah accept your efforts to get closer to Him.

UNIT 1
WHO IS ALLAH?

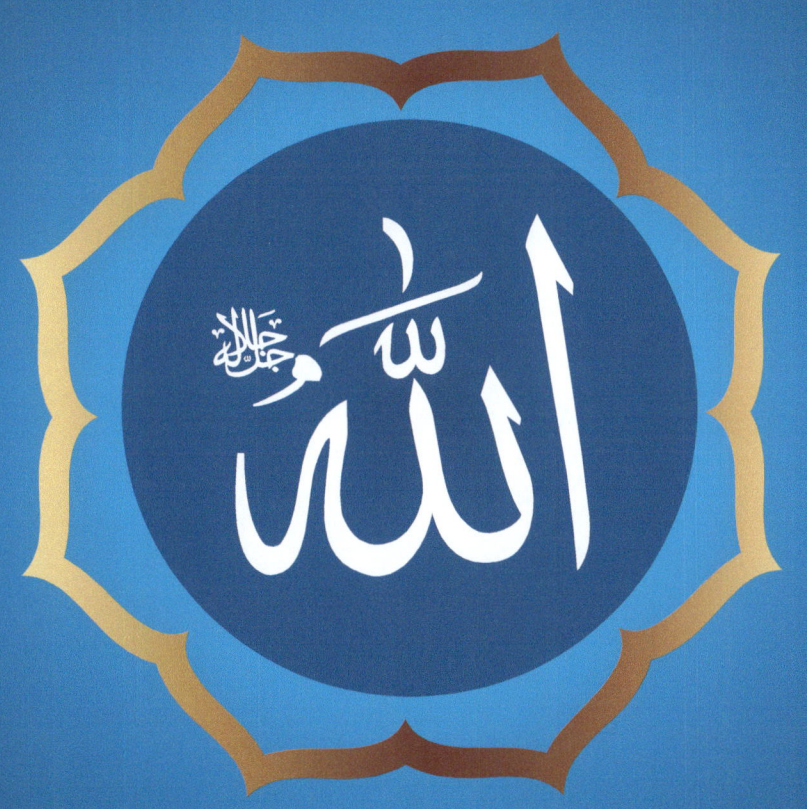

UNIT 1

Important Vocabulary

Al-A'laa
The Most High

Al-'Alee
The Most High and Exalted

Al-Fattah
The One who opens all closed doors

Al-Firdaws
The highest level of Paradise

Al-Ghafoor
The Most Forgiving

Al-Ghaffar
The One who forgives His servant over and over again

Al-Hafiz
The One who Protects

Al-Jabbar
The One whose control overtakes everyone else's

Al-Kareem
The Most Generous

Al-Mu'min
The One who provides security

Al-Muta'aal
The Supremely Exalted

Al-Mujeeb
The One who responds to our call

Al-Qadeer
The One Most Capable of doing all things

Al-Qahir
The Almighty, The Subduer

Al-Wadood
The Most Loving

Al-Wakeel
The One who takes care of our affairs in the best way

Ar-Raheem
The Most Merciful

Ar-Rahman
The Most Beneficent

Ar-Razzaq
The One who provides and sustains

Ash-Shakir
The Most Appreciative

Ash-Shakoor
The One Most ready to appreciate

At-Tawwab
The One who accepts repentance

Du'aa
Supplication

Rabb
Lord

Rahmah
Mercy

Ruboobiyyah
Lordship

Shirk
Ascribing partners with Allah

Ta'ib
Repentant

Tawassul
Taking the means to draw closer to Allah

Tawbah
Repentance

Tawheed
Allah's Oneness

Tawheed-ul-Asmaai was-Sifaat
Allah's Oneness in His Names and Attributes

Qadar
Divine Decree

TABLE OF CONTENTS

UNIT 1 | WHO IS ALLAH?

CHAPTER	PG	
01	11	Knowing Allah
02	21	Allah is Merciful
03	33	Allah Answers Me
04	49	Allah Forgives Me
05	63	Allah Appreciates Me
06	71	Allah Loves Me
07	79	Allah is The Most High
08	85	Allah is One

Essential Questions

This unit is designed to help answer the following questions.

1. Who is Allah?
2. Why is it important to know Allah?
3. How does knowing Allah's Names and Attributes affect my life?
4. Why guidelines are important in understanding the Name and Attributes of Allah?

▶ CHAPTER 1

KNOWING ALLAH

Tawheed-ul-Asmaai was-Sifaat
{ Allah's Oneness in His Names and Attributes }

If you were told, *"There's a lady called Mona; you should really love her and take all her advice."* Would you automatically start loving her and following her advice? Of course not! Why? It simply isn't possible to love someone you don't know. Love is an emotion, not simply a statement! If I start to give you detailed examples and incidents from her life that show her kindness, generosity, wisdom, strength, and patience, you would then begin to admire her and perhaps even feel your love towards her before even meeting her. You would definitely feel that this is someone you'd love to meet and get to know yourself. Let's say you were able to get to know her, and you confirmed that indeed she is as described. You got to know her by what she does and says in all situations and incidents you observe. The more time you spend with her and know her beautiful character traits, the more you'll love, respect, and admire her.

Why is it Important to Know Allah?

As mentioned in the previous example, it is not possible to love someone we don't know. Similarly, it is not possible to love Allah, as he deserves to be loved unless we know Him. But how is it possible to know someone we can't see - at least not yet? Allah has described Himself to us in many ways. He told us about His qualities, His names, and His actions, which are practical displays of His characteristics. He has spoken to us directly in the *Qur'an*, giving us an opportunity to get to know His characteristics through His speech. He has also manifested many of His qualities in His creation, as well as in His decrees and decisions (the various incidents that occur in our lives and the world around us).

Worship, as we will discuss later, is based on love and reverence. Therefore, it is extremely important for us to get to know Allah as He truly is in order for us to fulfill our purpose, sincere worship, and find fulfillment in that worship. In other words, if we know Allah well, we will love Him more than anyone else, obey Him with love and conviction, yearn to meet Him, and feel grateful to Him. This knowledge will fill our hearts with hope in Him alone, trust in Him alone, and fear of His disapproval alone; in other words, our hearts will be filled with *tawheed*. This aspect of *tawheed* (*Tawheed-ul-Asmaai was-Sifaat*) discusses the oneness of Allah in His Names and Attributes. Let us find out how the Oneness of Allah is maintained in His Names and Attributes as we explore further the guidelines used in understanding the Names and Attributes of Allah.

He is Allah,

other than whom there is no deity,

Knower of the unseen and the witnessed.

He is Entirely Merciful, the Especially Merciful.

He is Allah,

other than whom there is no deity,

the Sovereign, the Pure, the Perfection,

the Bestower of Faith, the Overseer, the Exalted in Might,

the Compeller, the Superior.

Exalted is Allah above whatever they associate with Him.

He is Allah,

the Creator, the Inventor, the Fashioner,

to Him belong the best names.

Whatever is in the heavens and earth is exalting Him.

And He is the Exalted in Might, the Wise.

_____

Surah Al-Hashr [59:22-24]

ARE YOU SAD OR WORRIED?

Prophet *sallAllahu 'alayhi wa sallam* prescribed the following *du'aa* as one of the treatments for sadness and worries.

He *sallAllahu 'alayhi wa sallam* said, "Whenever somebody is afflicted with worries and sadness and they say:

اللَّهُمَّ إِنِّي عَبْدُكَ، وَابْنُ عَبْدِكَ، وَابْنُ أَمَتِكَ، نَاصِيَتِي بِيَدِكَ، مَاضٍ فِيَّ حُكْمُكَ، عَدْلٌ فِيَّ قَضَاؤُكَ، أَسْأَلُكَ بِكُلِّ اسْمٍ هُوَ لَكَ، سَمَّيْتَ بِهِ نَفْسَكَ، أَوْ أَنْزَلْتَهُ فِي كِتَابِكَ، أَوْ عَلَّمْتَهُ أَحَدًا مِنْ خَلْقِكَ، أَوِ اسْتَأْثَرْتَ بِهِ فِي عِلْمِ الْغَيْبِ عِنْدَكَ، أَنْ تَجْعَلَ الْقُرْآنَ رَبِيعَ قَلْبِي، وَنُورَ صَدْرِي، وَجَلَاءَ حُزْنِي، وَذَهَابَ هَمِّي

'O Allah, I am Your slave, the son of Your male slave, the son of Your female slave. My forelock is in Your Hand, Your predestination is applying on me, and Your ruling regarding me is just. I ask You by every Name of Yours, that You name Yourself, taught to one of Your creation, sent in Your Book, or kept exclusive to knowledge of the unseen with You, to make the Qur'an the spring of my heart, the light of my chest, the removal of my sadness, and the thing that causes my worries to depart.'

Allah removes their sadness and worries and relieves them of their situation."

Say this du'aa often with all your heart reflecting on its meanings, and Allah will relieve your sadness and worries. [1]

---

1. Ahmad

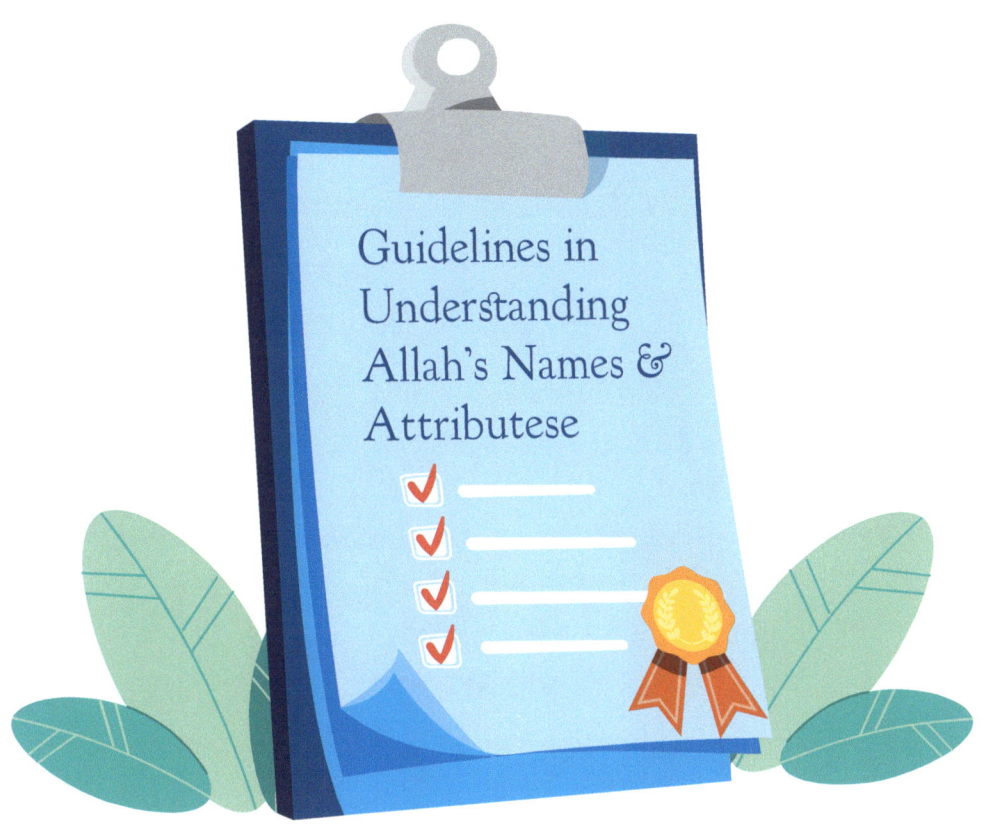

What Are The Guidelines in Understanding Allah's Names and Attributes?

Before we discuss this aspect of *tawheed* (maintaining Allah's Oneness in His Names and Attributes) and get to know more about Allah, it is important to establish how we are to understand His Names and Attributes. Because Allah is Divine, All-Powerful, and has no beginning or end, we will not comprehend everything about Him in human terms, simply because He is not human.

Allah said,

لَيْسَ كَمِثْلِهِ شَىْءٌ وَهُوَ ٱلسَّمِيعُ ٱلْبَصِيرُ

"Nothing is like Him, and He is the All-Hearing, the All-Seeing." [2]

> NOTHING IS LIKE HIM, AND HE IS THE ALL-HEARING, THE ALL-SEEING. [3]
>
> **Surah Ash-Shuraa**

---

2. Surah Ash-Shuraa [42:11]
3. Surah Ash-Shuraa [42:11]

THERE ARE A FEW IMPORTANT GUIDELINES WE MUST BEAR IN MIND AS WE LEARN ABOUT ALLAH'S NAMES AND ATTRIBUTES:

▶ ONE

Do not make up Names and Attributes that neither Allah nor His messenger *sallallahu 'alayhi wa sallam* **have mentioned in authenticated narrations**

We cannot guess what Allah is like based on our assumptions. We can only know Allah's names and characteristics based on what He told us. In other words, we cannot describe Him in a way with which He did not describe Himself or give Him new names or attributes that were not mentioned in the *Qur'an* or *hadith*. Likewise, we cannot negate or do away with a name or attribute He has informed us of. For example, we cannot call Allah "*Engineer of the Universe*," since He did not assign that name to Himself.

▶ TWO

Allah is perfect, do not liken Him to His creation

Although we have some qualities that Allah also has, His are perfect and unlimited, while ours are imperfect and limited. For example, Allah is living,z and we are also living, but His life is nothing like ours. He has no beginning or end, and we were born and will die. Allah hears, and we also hear, but our hearing is limited and His hearing is unlimited. He can hear everything, internal and external, silent and spoken, and He can hear everything at the same time. Our hearing is faulty, and His is perfect. Unlike us, He can't mishear anything. Allah speaks. For example, He spoke the *Qur'an* to Angel *Jibreel*, who revealed it to Prophet Muhammad *sallAllahu 'alayhi wa sallam*. He spoke to Musa *'alayhis salaam* and our Prophet *sallAllahu 'alayhi wa sallam* directly. He speaks to the angels. However, His speech is not like our speech. His is perfect, and ours is imperfect. His knowledge is infinite and perfect; ours is limited and imperfect, and so on. Similarly, we cannot attribute human weaknesses to Him. He is the Creator of the universe, so he does not need anything, be it sleep, food, support, help, company, or anything else.

▶ THREE

Do not interpret His Names and Attributes

We believe in and confirm the Names and Attributes He told us about without changing their meanings. For example, Allah says He has hands; we confirm that He has actual hands. We can't say, *"I think hands here symbolizes power because saying He has hands makes Him like His creation."* That's not what He said. When He says "power," He means power, and when He says "hands," He means hands. Otherwise, anyone can change the meaning of anything simply because he or she doesn't understand it. However, we know, based on the second principle, that His hands will be nothing like the hands of His creation. We also acknowledge that we cannot know what they look like or how they are because He did not inform us.

▶ FOUR

Allah's Attributes cannot be given to His creation

We cannot give the creation the attributes of Allah. For example, we cannot say that any creature knows everything, hears everything, sees everything, etc.

▶ FIVE

Allah's names cannot be given to anyone

We cannot call anyone else by the names of Allah. For example, one of Allah's names is *Al-Lateef* (the Most Subtle, the Most Gentle). We can name someone Abdul-Lateef (the servant of *Al-Lateef*) but not *Al-Lateef*. There are some qualities, like generosity or mercy, that we can refer to people by, but in this case, we will remove the article *"Al (the)."* For example, from Allah's names are *Ar-Raheem* (The Most Merciful) and *Al-Kareem* (The Most Generous). We can name someone simply *Raheem* (merciful) or *Kareem* (generous).

▶ SIX

Negative attributes are not assigned to Allah

We cannot assign negative attributes such as *Al-Muntaqim* (the Avenger) to Allah.

DID YOU KNOW?

There are certain names that we cannot assign to anyone. These are specific only to Allah. We should not assign or call someone these names even if the definite article Al (the) is removed from these names. These names can only be used when preceded by the word "*Abd*" (servant).

THESE NAMES ARE AS FOLLOWS: [4]

Allah
Ar-Rabb
Ar-Rahman
The Most Merciful

As-Samad
The Eternal, Satisfier of Needs

Al-Ahad
The Unique, The Only One

Al-Mutakabbir
The Supreme, The Majestic

SOME SCHOLARS ALSO ADD THE FOLLOWING NAMES:

Al-Khaaliq
The Creator, The Maker

Ar-Razzaq
The Provider

'Allaamul Ghayb
Knower of the Unseen

Al-Awwal
The First

Al-Akhir
The Last

Al-Baatin
The Hidden One, The Knower of the Hidden

Al-Qaahir
The Subduer, The Ever Dominating

Al-Jabbar
Resolver of the affairs of all creatures

Ad-Dhaahir
The Manifest

---
4. According to the majority of scholars.

REMEBER

- ✖ **DO NOT** GIVE HIM NAMES AND ATTRIBUTES
- ✖ **DO NOT** COMPARE HIM TO HIS CREATION
- ✖ **DO NOT** INTERPRET HIS NAMES AND ATTRIBUTES
- ✖ **DO NOT** GIVE ALLAH'S ATTRIBUTES TO HIS CREATION
- ✖ **DO NOT** GIVE ALLAH'S NAMES TO ANYONE
- ✖ **DO NOT** ASSIGN NEGATIVE ATTRIBUTES TO ALLAH

CHAPTER 1
REVIEW AND REFLECT QUESTIONS

1. How does learning more about Allah's Names and Attributes help us come closer to him in our daily lives?

2. Allah has given His servants so many names to call Him and supplicate with. What do you understand about this? What would be the difference if He only shared with us a few Names and Attributes of His?

3. Contemplate what kind of challenges you have in your life today. Which Names and Attributes of Allah come to your mind when trying to seek Allah's help?

4. If you love someone, do you want to know everything about them? What steps can you take to strengthen your love and understanding of Allah?

5. What is the appropriate response to the following scenarios?:

a. In the Bible, it is mentioned that God created the heavens and the earth in six days and then He rested on the seventh day. So God blessed the 7th day and made it holy because on it God rested from all His work that He had done in creation. Therefore, some members of the Christian and Jewish faiths do not work on Saturday or Sunday. Knowing Allah's Names and Attributes, what would you say to a Muslim friend who has picked up this concept from his non-Muslim friends and says, *"Allah rested on the seventh day."*

b. Your friend just came across the ayah in the Qur'an, *"The entire Earth will be in His (hand's) grip on the Day of Resurrection, and the heavens will be folded in His right hand."* Az-Zumar [39:67] She starts to contemplate what Allah's hands look like and what they mean to her. What information do you think is relevant for her to know about Allah's hands?

c. Knowing Allah's Names and Attributes What would you say to someone who says, *"I am the greatest (Al-Akbar)"* or *"I am the most knowledgeable (Al-'Aleem)"*?

d. Your friend's name is Abdur-Rahman. Should his name be shortened to Rahman? How about *"Ramy"*?

CHAPTER 2

 &

Ar-Rahman
{ The Most Beneficent }

Ar-Raheem
{ The Most Merciful }

ALLAH IS MERCIFUL

Both of these names can be translated as *"The Most Merciful."* However, in Arabic, **Ar-Rahman** indicates that mercy is part of Allah's nature, while **Ar-Raheem** indicates that He is merciful in His actions, that is, that He imparts this mercy to His creation. Allah has given these two names special importance. He began the entire *Qur'an*, as well as each *surah*, with these names (In the Name of Allah, *Ar-Rahman, Ar-Raheem*).

A person's mercy is a drop in an ocean compared to Allah's mercy and kindness.

The Prophet *sallAllahu 'alayhi wa sallam* explained this by saying,

"There are one hundred (parts of) Allah's mercy. He has sent down one part of this mercy (and spread it) among the jinn, humans, animals, and insects, and it is because of this (one part) that they love one another and show kindness to one another, such that even a wild animal treats its young one with affection. Allah has reserved ninety-nine parts of mercy with which He will treat His servants on the Day of Resurrection." [5]

---

5. Sahih Muslim

"There are one hundred (parts of) Allah's mercy. He has sent down one part of this mercy (and spread it) among the jinn, humans, animals, and insects, and it is because of this (one part) that they love one another and show kindness to one another, such that even a wild animal treats its young one with affection. Allah has reserved ninety-nine parts of mercy with which He will treat His servants on the Day of Resurrection." [6]

―――――――――――――――――――

6. Sahih Muslim

The Prophet *sallAllahu 'alayhi wa sallam* once saw a woman searching frantically for her young child, and as soon as she found him, she embraced him and began nursing him. The Prophet *sallAllahu 'alayhi wa sallam* then turned to his companions and said, *"Can you ever imagine this woman throwing her child in a fire?"* They responded, *"We swear by Allah, she would never throw him in a fire as long as it's within her capability!"* The Prophet *sallAllahu 'alayhi wa sallam* then said, *"And Allah is most certainly more merciful to His servant than this woman is to her child."* [7]

He also informed us that His mercy is so great that it precedes His anger. Allah's Messenger *sallAllahu 'alayhi wa sallam* said, *"When Allah created the creations, He wrote with Him on His Throne: 'My mercy has preceded My anger.'"* [8]

General Mercy

Allah has a general mercy for all His creation, believers and disbelievers alike. He does not even deprive those who disbelieve in Him of His blessings, even though it is within His power to do so. He grants all His creations countless blessings and provisions, such as health (including the ability to eat, drink, and breathe), wealth, family, and security.

Allah says,

وَمِن رَّحْمَتِهِ جَعَلَ لَكُمُ ٱلَّيْلَ وَٱلنَّهَارَ لِتَسْكُنُوا۟ فِيهِ وَلِتَبْتَغُوا۟ مِن فَضْلِهِ وَلَعَلَّكُمْ تَشْكُرُونَ

"And out of His mercy He made for you the night and the day that you may rest therein and [by day] seek from His bounty and [that] perhaps you will be grateful." [9]

His mercy prevents Him from punishing people immediately when they reject Him. Rather, He continues to send people His signs and grants them countless chances to come back to Him, time and time again.

Special Mercy

Allah also has a special mercy for His believing servants in this life as well as the next. He explained this type of mercy (*rahmah*) in His statement,

وَكَانَ بِٱلْمُؤْمِنِينَ رَحِيمًا

"And truly, He is ever so Merciful with the believers." [10]

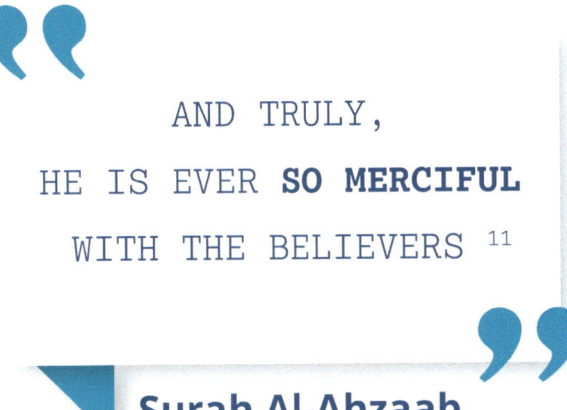

AND TRULY, HE IS EVER **SO MERCIFUL** WITH THE BELIEVERS [11]

Surah Al-Ahzaab

---

7. Sahih Muslim
8. Sahih Al-Bukhari
9. Surah Al-Qasas [28:73]
10. Surah Al-Ahzaab [33:43]
11. Surah Al-Ahzaab [33:43]

EXAMPLES OF ALLAH'S SPECIAL MERCY

This special mercy comes in many forms, and below are a few examples:

▶ ONE
Allah Answers Our *Du'aas* (supplications)

As we learned earlier, He granted Prophet Zakariyyah *'alayhis salaam* a child when he and his wife had become elderly, and it was "impossible" in medical terms for them to conceive a child. He grants us what we need and want even without our asking.

▶ TWO
He Protects us

From His mercy, He protects us from what we fear in the future. Think of how many times you were afraid of something in the future that might happen, and it never did because Allah protected you. This is why Prophet Ya'qub *'alayhis salaam* said,

فَاللَّهُ خَيْرٌ حَافِظًا وَهُوَ أَرْحَمُ ٱلرَّٰحِمِينَ

"Allah is the best protector, and He is the Most Merciful of all those who are merciful." [12]

He mentioned His overpowering mercy in context of His protection to show that because He is immensely merciful, He will protect us from what we fear. Similarly, when Angel Jibreel *'alayhis salaam* walked in on Maryam *'alayhas salaam* in the form of a man, she was naturally afraid of the perceived stranger. She immediately asked Allah to protect her from harm out of His infinite mercy:

قَالَتْ إِنِّي أَعُوذُ بِٱلرَّحْمَٰنِ مِنكَ إِن كُنتَ تَقِيًّا

"I seek protection from Ar-Rahman (the Most Merciful) from you _ " [13]

That is, because He is the Most Merciful, He will protect us from what we fear.

---

12. Surah Yusuf [12:64]
13. Surah Maryam [19:18]

▶ THREE
He Guides Us to Him

Out of His vast mercy, He guides us to Him, even in times when we are not seeking it. You may find that you unintentionally come across a friend, a lecture, an article, a book, or even an incident that becomes a source of guidance for you at the right exact moment.

▶ FOUR
He Calms Us

Out of His kindness, mercy, and compassion, He reassures us and puts peace in our hearts in our times of fear or sorrow. Another example of the Most Merciful providing comfort and assurance to His beloved servants is in the story of Yusuf *'alayhis salaam*. When his brothers ruthlessly threw him in a well, you can only imagine the fear and pain he felt as a young child. Although normally Allah sends His revelation to prophets in adulthood, He quickly sent Yusuf a revelation saying,

وَأَوْحَيْنَا إِلَيْهِ لَتُنَبِّئَنَّهُم بِأَمْرِهِمْ هَٰذَا وَهُمْ لَا يَشْعُرُونَ

"But We revealed to him, 'You will surely inform them [someday] about this affair of theirs while they do not perceive [your identity].'" [14]

This reassured him of several comforting facts: that he would live through this and eventually reunite with his family.

---
14. Surah Yusuf [12:15]

▶ FIVE

He Forgives Us

Because of His mercy, He opened the door of repentance, no matter how major the sin is or how often it was done. One of Allah's names is *At-Tawwab* (the One who accepts repentance).

▶ SIX

Allah's mercy in our hardships and trials

His mercy is even evident in our hardships and trials. We begin Surah *Al-Fatiha* with the statement,

ٱلْحَمْدُ لِلَّهِ رَبِّ ٱلْعَٰلَمِينَ ٱلرَّحْمَٰنِ ٱلرَّحِيمِ

"Praise be to Allah, the Rabb of the worlds, Ar-Rahman, Ar-Raheem." [15]

He made a connection between His *Ruboobiyyah* (Lordship) and His mercy to show that whatever He causes to happen (*ruboobiyyah*) is out of His mercy, even if it appears to be bad. We discussed the example of Khidr *'alayhis salaam* and Prophet Musa *'alayhis salaam* when we spoke about *Tawheed ur-Ruboobiyyah*.

▶ SEVEN

Mercy for the believers on the Day of Judgment

Although the Day of Judgment is equivalent to 50,000 years, Allah will make it easy, light, and short for the believers. The Prophet *sallAllahu 'alayhi wa sallam* said, **"The Day of Judgment, for the believer, will be like the time between Dhuhr and Asr."** [16]

His mercy will be the cause of His vast forgiveness on that Day and will cause the believers to live in eternal bliss in Paradise.

---

15. Surah Al-Fatihah [1:2-3]
16. Al-Hakim

▶ EIGHT

Allah sent the *Qur'an* as a mercy to mankind

He states,

ٱلرَّحْمَٰنُ
عَلَّمَ ٱلْقُرْءَانَ
خَلَقَ ٱلْإِنسَٰنَ
عَلَّمَهُ ٱلْبَيَانَ

"The Most Merciful. He taught the Qur'an, created the human, and taught him eloquence." [17]

The first blessing He mentioned after informing us that He is the Most Merciful is that He taught us the *Qur'an*, indicating that revealing the *Qur'an* is among His greatest acts of mercy.

He also said,

وَنَزَّلْنَا عَلَيْكَ ٱلْكِتَٰبَ تِبْيَٰنًا لِّكُلِّ شَىْءٍ وَهُدًى وَرَحْمَةً وَبُشْرَىٰ لِلْمُسْلِمِينَ

"And We revealed the Book to you, as a clarification of everything, as well as a guidance, mercy, and glad tidings for those who submit." [18]

With the *Qur'an*, Allah liberated us from the worship of others besides Him. The *Qur'an* guides us from darkness into light, from confusion to clarity, from ignorance to knowledge, and from misery in this life and the next to happiness in both worlds.

▶ NINE

He Placed Mercy Among Us

From His mercy, He placed mercy between His servants and instructed us to be merciful to one another. The prophet *sallAllahu 'alayhi wa sallam* said,

"Ar-Rahman will show mercy to those who are merciful. Be merciful to those on the earth and the One above the heavens will be merciful to you." [19]

---

17. Surah Ar-Rahmaan [55:1-4]
18. Surah An-Nahl [16:89]
19. At-Tirmidhi and Abu Dawood

EFFECTS OF KNOWING AR-RAHMAN & AR-RAHEEM ON MY LIFE

These names and qualities help us to know Allah better and in a way that will affect our hearts and future actions, some of which are as follows:

1

IT INCREASES OUR LOVE FOR ALLAH

Because His mercy for us is unlike that of anyone else, our love for Him is naturally stronger than our love of anyone else.

2

WE WILL ASK FOR ALLAH'S MERCY

As the prophets *'alayhimus salaam* did. For example, Musa *'alayhis salaam* said,

وَأَدْخِلْنَا فِى رَحْمَتِكَ وَأَنتَ أَرْحَمُ ٱلرَّٰحِمِينَ

"And enter us into Your mercy, truly, You are the most Merciful from all those who are merciful." [20]

3

IT REMOVES HOPELESSNESS OR DESPAIR

By understanding Allah's mercy, we will not feel hopelessness and despair. We have hope that He will answer our *du'aas*, that He will forgive our sins, and that, in the end, everything will turn out for the best.

---

20. Surah Al-'Araf [7:151]

4

IT WILL MAKE US MORE MERCIFUL AND COMPASSIONATE

We ourselves will be more merciful and compassionate to everyone: our parents, siblings, relatives, friends, the needy, strangers, and animals. This mercy will cause us to speak kind words, to put ourselves in other people's shoes, to be tolerant of others' mistakes, and to treat others as we would like to be treated.

5

WE WILL BE DILIGENT TO PRACTICE THE *QUR'AN* AND THE *SUNNAH*

We will want to strive to learn, understand, and apply the *Qur'an* and the *Sunnah* to get the most mercy we can out of them.

6

WE WILL LEAD FULFILLING LIVES

We will lead more fulfilling lives by obeying Allah's commands and leaving what He prohibited us to do because we know these rules are a source of mercy.

7

WE WILL BE SHY TO DISOBEY ALLAH

We will be shy to disobey or displease Allah after He has shown us such great mercy. When a person is extremely kind, generous, and merciful to us, we feel embarrassed to disappoint them. So how much more should we feel this shyness towards Allah?

CHAPTER 2
REVIEW AND REFLECT QUESTIONS

1

"How can Allah do this to me! Doesn't He have any mercy for me?" You hear someone say that when they are going through a traumatic or challenging situation. Knowing Allah is *Ar-Rahman* and *Ar-Raheem*, how would you explain to them that Allah's mercy is in fact still present even in their difficult situation?

2

Knowing that Allah is merciful with us when we make mistakes and does not punish us immediately. How can we transform our thought process when our feelings are hurt by someone from seeking to retaliate to forgiving?

3

Yusuf prepared a lunch bag for his afternoon sports class. When he got to the class, he saw his friend was tired and forgot his lunch bag at home. Yusuf reaches into his lunch bag, splits his sandwich in half, and opens up his banana and does the same. What does this tell you about Yusuf's attentiveness and mercy to others? Have you been in a situation where you were given the same opportunity?

CHAPTER 3

Al-Mujeeb
{ The One who responds to our *du'aa* (call) }

ALLAH ANSWERS ME

Allah says,

فَٱسْتَغْفِرُوهُ ثُمَّ تُوبُوٓا۟ إِلَيْهِ إِنَّ رَبِّى قَرِيبٌ مُّجِيبٌ

"So ask his forgiveness, then repent to Him. Truly, my Rabb is Qareeb (Most Near), Mujeeb (the One who responds)." [21]

Al-Mujeeb is the only ONE who hears the *du'aa* of those who call ON HIM and responds to them by granting them what they are asking.

He also says,

أَمَّن يُجِيبُ ٱلْمُضْطَرَّ إِذَا دَعَاهُ وَيَكْشِفُ ٱلسُّوٓءَ وَيَجْعَلُكُمْ خُلَفَآءَ ٱلْأَرْضِ أَءِلَـٰهٌ مَّعَ ٱللَّهِ قَلِيلًا مَّا تَذَكَّرُونَ

"Say: who answers the *du'aa* (call) of the desperate one when he calls on Him and who removes his affliction? (So) is there any other god besides Allah? Yet you hardly remember!" [22]

 BRAIN TEASER

What is Allah asking from us in the following *ayah*?

وَإِذَا سَأَلَكَ عِبَادِى عَنِّى فَإِنِّى قَرِيبٌ أُجِيبُ دَعْوَةَ ٱلدَّاعِ إِذَا دَعَانِ فَلْيَسْتَجِيبُوا۟ لِى وَلْيُؤْمِنُوا۟ بِى لَعَلَّهُمْ يَرْشُدُونَ

"And if my servants ask you about Me, (inform them that) certainly, I am near: I answer the *du'aa* (call) of the one who asks when he asks. So let them respond to Me and believe in Me so that they may be rightly guided." [23]

---

21. Surah Hud [11:61]
22. Surah An-Naml [27:62]
23. Surah Al-Baqarah [2:186]

What Does This Mean in My Life?

FROM THE NAME OF ALLAH *AL-MUJEEB* WE UNDERSTAND THAT:

1 ALLAH DOES NOT GET UPSET WHEN YOU ASK HIM

Like all His other traits, Allah's trait of granting our requests is the most complete and perfect, and no one can compare to Him. So even though people may be willing to help us or grant us some requests, if we ask too much or become too dependent, they start to get annoyed. However, when it comes to Allah, the Prophet *sallAllahu 'alayhi wa sallam* said regarding Allah,

"If someone does not ask Allah, Allah gets angry at him." [24] He *sallAllahu 'alayhi wa sallam* also stated, *"The most miserly person is the one who is too miserly to give salams, and the most incapable (or feeble) person is the one who fails to make du'aa."* [25]

2 ALLAH'S LOVE IS INFINITE

Mercy, love, and compassion of people are limited, whereas these traits in Allah are infinite and perfect. Allah is the only one who is the Most Merciful and Most Loving.

3 ALLAH IS CAPABLE OF EVERYTHING

Even if people would sincerely like to help us, their abilities and capacities are limited. A person cannot **ultimately** grant us health and well-being, remove sickness, protect us from disasters, grant us a happy marriage, guide us or our loved ones, grant us success in our studies or careers, or increase our wealth, or fulfill any other such wishes. However, Allah is the **only** one who is Most Powerful and Most Able to do all things *(Al-Qadeer)*. He is the **only** Owner of everything that exists *(Malik Al-Mulk)* and can give and withhold as He wishes.

4 ALLAH DOES NOT HUMILIATE YOU WHEN YOU ASK HIM

People may expect something in return or one day remind the person that they helped them. Therefore, dependence on people and asking them too much can be a humiliating experience, whereas humbleness and humility before Allah are a means of dignity and emotional independence from others.

---

24. At-Tirmidhi
25. Ibn Hibban

Allah Loves *Du'aa*

Even though we are the ones asking and Allah is the one giving, He loves for us to call on him. *Du'aa* is an act of obedience and worship that brings us closer to Allah. This is why our Prophet *sallAllahu 'alayhi wa sallam* said, *"Du'aa is worship."* He *sallAllahu 'alayhi wa sallam* also said, *"Truly, Allah is shy and generous. When His servant raises his hands to ask him, He is shy to return them empty."* [26]

There is No Limit on How Much a Person Can Ask

The Prophet *sallAllahu 'alayhi wa sallam* said, *"If any of you makes du'aa, don't say, 'O Allah, forgive me if you wish.' Rather, let him be determined in his request and greatly desire, making his wishes great. For, truly, nothing is too great for Allah to give."* [27]

The Prophet *sallAllahu 'alayhi wa sallam* also said in this regard, *"When one of you makes du'aa for something, let him be plentiful (in what he asks for), for truly, he is asking his Lord."* [28]

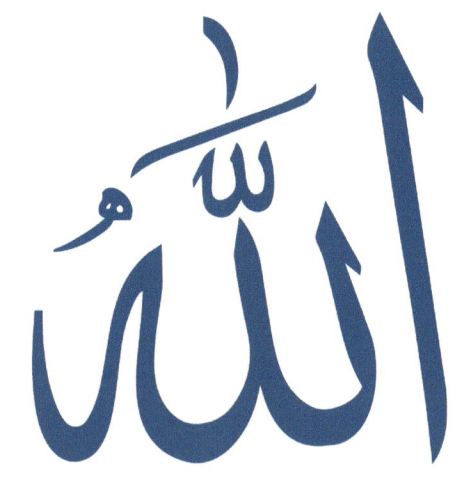

Why Does Allah Love it When You Make *Du'aa*?

Du'aa demonstrates that we truly believe that we have a Lord who is the Most Merciful, Most Loving, and Most Generous, who hears us when no one else can and who responds to us. It shows our belief that He is the only one who owns and controls everything in the universe, and thus, He is the only one who can grant us our wishes, bring us what is beneficial, repel what is harmful, and protect us from what we fear.

Due to the greatness of this act of worship, Allah has made it so powerful that He can cause it to change our divine decree! The Prophet *sallAllahu 'alayhi wa sallam* said, *"Nothing repels qadar (divine decree) except du'aa."* [29]

---

26. At-Tirmidhi, Ibn Hibban
27. Sahih Muslim
28. Ibn Hibban
29. Al-Hakim

Journey to Allah Series *Who Is Allah?* | 35

ALLAH'S RESPONSE TO OUR DU'AAS

1. HE WILL GRANT IT

If our request is something beneficial for us, Allah will often respond by giving us what we asked for right away.

2. HE MAY DELAY IT

In His infinite knowledge and wisdom, He may delay it because this is not the best timing and instead grant it to us at another time. If it is not best for us, even if we don't understand why, Allah may not grant us our request but instead cause it to remove an affliction that was about to occur, thereby protecting us from harm and devastation.

3. HE MAY SAVE IT AS A REWARD FOR US

If He does not answer our *du'aa* directly in this world, He may save it for us in the form of reward on the Day of Judgment, when we will be in desperate need of any reward we can get. At that time, we will feel grateful to know that it was not given in the *dunya* but reserved for the Hereafter.

The Prophet *sallAllahu 'alayhi wa sallam* said, *"Whenever any Muslim makes a du'aa, as long as it does not involve sin or cutting family ties, Allah will give him one of three things: He will get his du'aa right away (i.e., in the dunya), it will be saved for him in the Hereafter, or it will repel a similar evil from befalling him."* The sahabah asked, *"So should we increase our du'aa?"* He said, *"Yes, increase."* [30]

---

30. Ahmad, Al-Hakim

CONDITIONS FOR *DU'AAS* TO BE ACCEPTED...

TAWHEED
Knowing and believing that ONLY Allah can answer our *du'aa* and grant us what we want, remove what pains us, or protect us from what we fear.

SINCERITY
When we make *du'aa*, it should be a sincere act of worship for Allah alone, not to show off or gain people's approval.

PATIENCE
When we make *du'aa*, we must be patient and not lose hope or complain that our du'aa is not being answered. The Prophet *sallAllahu 'alayhi wa sallam* said, *"The du'aa of the (Allah's) servant will continue to be answered as long as he is not hasty by saying, 'I have prayed and prayed, but my du'aa was not answered.'"* [31]

HALAL INCOME
For *du'aa* to be accepted, a person's provisions and wealth, such as his food, drink, clothing, etc., should come from halal sources, according to a *hadith*.

CERTAINTY & ATTENTIVE HEART
"...Make du'aa to Allah while you are certain your du'aa will be accepted..." (At-Tirmidhi). We must be intentional and mindful in our *du'aa*. We have to be attentive and do so sincerely from our hearts.

DU'AA FOR GOOD THINGS
A person cannot make *du'aa* for sins or for something that will bring harm to himself or others.

---
31. Sahih Al-Bukhari and Sahih Muslim

TAWHEED
(in the heart)

This means knowing that Allah - and ONLY Allah - can answer our *du'aa* and grant us what we want, remove what pains us, or protect us from what we fear. It also includes believing that He is *Al-Mujeeb* and that He will indeed answer our *du'aas*.

SINCERITY

When we make *du'aa*, it should be a sincere act of worship for Allah alone, not to show off or gain people's approval. An example of this is when someone is in the *masjid* and the imam comes in, so he lifts his hands and increases his *du'aa* so he will impress the imam. This negates any righteous action that is not done purely for the sake of Allah. As Allah tells us,

فَٱدْعُوا ٱللَّهَ مُخْلِصِينَ لَهُ ٱلدِّينَ وَلَوْ كَرِهَ ٱلْكَٰفِرُونَ

"So call upon Allah with sincere devotion, even if the disbelievers dislike it." [32]

PATIENCE

When we make *du'aa,* we must be patient and not lose hope or complain that our du'aa is not being answered.

DU'AA FOR GOOD THINGS

A person cannot make *du'aa* for sins or for something that will bring harm to himself or others. The Prophet *sallAllahu 'alayhi wa sallam* said, *"Whenever any Muslim makes a du'aa, as long as it does not involve sin or cutting family ties, Allah will give him one of three things..."* [33]

---

32. Surah Ghaafir [40:14]
33. Ahmad, Al-Hakim

NOT CONSUMING HARAM FOOD & DRINK

CERTAINTY & AN ATTENTIVE HEART

When we make *du'aa*, we have to make sure it is not mere lip service. We have to be attentive and do so sincerely from our hearts. A person may mumble, *"O Allah forgive me,"* after *salah* as a routine and habit without concentrating or thinking about what he is saying. This is not true *du'aa*. We must be intentional and mindful in our *du'aa*.

The Prophet sallAllahu 'alayhi wa sallam said, *"Make du'aa to Allah while you are certain your du'aa will be accepted. And know that Allah does not respond to a du'aa that comes from a negligent, inattentive heart."* [34]

HALAL INCOME

Such things as food and wealth must come from halal sources. The Prophet sallAllahu 'alayhi wa sallam mentioned a traveler on a long journey, disheveled and dusty. This situation indicates someone who is humble and in need, someone whom Allah would normally respond to.

He said, *"He stretches his hands to the sky and asks, 'O Lord! O Lord!' But his food is haram, his drink is haram, his clothing is haram, and he is nourished with haram. So how can his du'aa possibly be answered?"* [35]

---

34. At-Tirmidhi
35. Sahih Muslim

Etiquettes of Making *Du'aa*

1. Praise Allah
2. Send the *Salah* on the Prophet sallallahu 'Alayhi wa sallam.
3. Make *Du'aa* in Good Times and in Hard Times.
4. Ask for Everything, Small or Great.

ETIQUETTE #1

Praise Allah before the *du'aa* using Allah's beautiful Names and Attributes. Choose the name that suits your *du'aa*. For example, if you are asking for a job that will increase your income, ask Allah by His name *Ar-Razzaq* (The Provider) and *Al-Kareem* (The Most Generous). If you are asking for you or your loved one to be cured, ask Allah by His name *Ash-Shafi*, and so on. Allah said,

وَلِلَّهِ ٱلْأَسْمَآءُ ٱلْحُسْنَىٰ فَٱدْعُوهُ بِهَا

"And to Allah belong the most beautiful Names, so make *du'aa* to Him with them." 36

ETIQUETTE #2

Send prayers upon the Prophet *sallAllahu 'alayhi wa sallam*. The Prophet *sallAllahu 'alayhi wa sallam* heard one of the companions saying,

"O Allah, forgive me and have mercy on me." So he said, "He was hasty." Then he called him and resumed, "When any of you finishes your salah, start with the exaltation and praise of Allah, then send prayers upon the Prophet, and then after that, make du'aa for whatever you wish." 37

ETIQUETTE #3

Don't make *du'aa* only in difficult times, but also in good times. The Prophet *sallAllahu 'alayhi wa sallam* said, "Whoever wishes that Allah responds to his du'aa at times of hardship, then let him increase his du'aa in times of ease." 38

ETIQUETTE #4

Make *du'aa* for everything: big and small things regarding matters of both *deen* and *dunya*. Allah says,

وَمِنْهُم مَّن يَقُولُ رَبَّنَآ ءَاتِنَا فِى ٱلدُّنْيَا حَسَنَةً وَفِى ٱلْءَاخِرَةِ حَسَنَةً وَقِنَا عَذَابَ ٱلنَّارِ

"And there are those who say, 'Our rabb, give us good in the dunya and good in the akhirah, and save us from the Fire.'" 39

He also said,

ٱدْعُوا۟ رَبَّكُمْ تَضَرُّعًا وَخُفْيَةً إِنَّهُۥ لَا يُحِبُّ ٱلْمُعْتَدِينَ

"Call on your Lord with humility and in secret. Truly, He does not like the transgressors." *

---

36. Surah Al-A'raaf [7:180]
37. Abu Dawood
38. At-Tirmidhi
39. Surah Al-Baqarah [2:201]
*. Surah Al-A'raaf [7:55]

How to Increase the Chances of Our *Du'aas* being Accepted?

In order to increase the chances of our *du'aas* being accepted, we can take the means to draw closer to Allah (*Tawassul*). **Tawassul** means to take a means between the person and Allah to bring him / her closer to Him. This means it can be by acts of worship that Allah loves and that which pleases Him.

✗ STAY AWAY FROM ✗ THIS TYPE OF TAWASSUL

There is a type of *tawassul*, which is *shirk*, and that is to call on someone as a "*middleperson*" between the person and Allah, hoping that this will increase a person's chances of having their *du'aa* accepted. This would include, for example, asking or praying to a prophet, an angel, or a righteous dead person, asking them to deliver your *du'aas* to Allah or help you get your *du'aas* accepted. This is a form of major *shirk*.

The few recommended tawassul means that will indeed increase our chances of having our du'aas accepted are:

1. ASK ALLAH BY HIS NAMES AND ATTRIBUTES

Allah said,

وَلِلَّهِ ٱلْأَسْمَاءُ ٱلْحُسْنَىٰ فَٱدْعُوهُ بِهَا

"And to Allah belong the most beautiful Names and Attributes, so call on Him using them." [40]

All the *du'aas* mentioned in the *Qur'an* demonstrate this. Furthermore, we must choose the name that is suitable for our request. For example, we can ask Allah for any favors using names like *Ar-Rahman* (the Most Merciful) or *Al-Kareem* (the Most Generous). More specifically, when we ask for forgiveness, we can call on Him by *Al-Ghafoor* (the Most Forgiving) and *At-Tawwab* (the One who guides to repentance and accepts it). We can ask him to provide us with wealth, a good job, a righteous spouse, good friends, or anything of benefit using the name *Ar-Razzaq*. We can ask Him to guide us and our loved ones using the name or attribute of *Al-Hady* (the One who guides), and we can implore Him to cure us or our loved ones with the name *Ash-Shafi*.

---

40. Surah Al-A'raaf [7:180]

 **ACTIVITY** When can you use the following names of Allah?

AL-HAFIZ

AL-WAKEEL

AL-MU'MIN

AL-FATTAH

AL-JABBAR

AL-WADOOD

1. **AL-HAFIZ** (the One who protects)
2. **AL-WAKEEL** (the One who takes care of our affairs in the best way)
3. **AL-MU'MIN** (the One who provides security)
4. **AL-JABBAR** (the One who mends what is broken, or the One whose control overtakes everyone else's)
5. **AL-WADOOD** (the Most loving)
6. **AL-FATTAH** (the One who opens all closed doors and means)

2. MENTION ALLAH'S FAVORS

Allah said,

وَإِذْ تَأَذَّنَ رَبُّكُمْ لَئِن شَكَرْتُمْ لَأَزِيدَنَّكُمْ ۖ وَلَئِن كَفَرْتُمْ إِنَّ عَذَابِي لَشَدِيدٌ

"And [remember] when your Lord proclaimed, 'If you are grateful, I will certainly give you more. But if you are ungrateful, surely My punishment is severe.'" [41]

So, before asking Allah to give us more, we should remember how much He has already given us and thank Him for these blessings. This will cause Allah to give us more by answering our *du'aas*.

3. HUMBLY SHOW YOUR DESPERATE NEED FOR ALLAH

We can do this by detailing the state we are in and asking for Allah's mercy. Although Allah already knows our situation, when we explain it in detail, we show utmost need and desperation for Allah, which are signs of true submission to Him and belief in His power and mercy.

4. MENTION THE POSITIVE EFFECTS OF YOUR *DU'AA*

For example, if you are asking Allah to cure a sickness, mention the positive ways you can use your good health. If you ask Allah for righteous children, mention how they can serve His religion. An example of this can be seen in the Prophet's sallAllahu 'alayhi wa sallam statement, *"When a person comes to visit the sick, let him say, 'O Allah, cure Your servant So-and-so, for he will then hurt the enemy (in battle) or walk for your sake to the prayer.'"* [42] Another example is when Prophet Ibrahim 'alayhis salaam left his wife Hajar and son Ismail in the desert. He made *du'aa* saying,

رَّبَّنَا إِنِّي أَسْكَنتُ مِن ذُرِّيَّتِي بِوَادٍ غَيْرِ ذِي زَرْعٍ عِندَ بَيْتِكَ الْمُحَرَّمِ رَبَّنَا لِيُقِيمُوا الصَّلَوٰةَ فَاجْعَلْ أَفْئِدَةً مِّنَ النَّاسِ تَهْوِي إِلَيْهِمْ وَارْزُقْهُم مِّنَ الثَّمَرَٰتِ لَعَلَّهُمْ يَشْكُرُونَ

"O my Lord! I have left my family to live in a valley that has no fruits, close to your Sacred House, so that they may establish the prayer. Our Lord! So cause a group of people to love them and provide them with fruits so that they may show gratitude." [43]

---

41. Surah Ibrahim [14:7]
42. Abu Dawood
43. Surah Ibrahim [14:37]

5. ASK ALLAH BY MENTIONING GOOD DEEDS THAT YOU'VE DONE PURELY FOR HIS SAKE

Note that when you did the good deed, you did not do it for Allah to give you something specific; you had done it purely for His sake. However, when you are in a situation of need, you can remember this deed and mention it as a cause for Allah to accept your *du'aa*.

This is clearly illustrated in the following story narrated by the Prophet *sallAllahu 'alayhi wa sallam*, in which three men were stuck in a cave with a boulder blocking its exit. They decided to each ask Allah with a good deed they had done purely for Allah's sake. One of them mentioned that, upon his return from herding his animals, he would always feed his parents milk before his wife and children. One day, they were asleep, and he did not want to disturb them, so he waited with the milk by their side until they awakened, while his children were by his side crying for some of the milk. He concluded, saying, *"O Allah! If You know that I did this for Your sake, then please remove this rock,"* and the rock moved a little. The second mentioned a time when he was deeply in love with his cousin, who refused to accept his request for an illegitimate relationship unless he gave her a huge sum of money. He worked hard to get this money, and when he was about to fulfill his desire with her, she admonished him to fear Allah and not to have a relationship with her except by marriage. So he got up and left her. He also concluded with the same *du'aa* that the first man and the rock moved a little more. The third man mentioned an employee of his who once refused to take his payment and left. He invested his payment, buying many cows and a shepherd. When the man eventually came and demanded his money, he gave him all the cattle and the shepherd, much to the man's surprise. He also concluded with the *du'aa*, *"O Allah! If you know I did this for your sake, then please remove the rock."* And the rock moved completely, opening the cave's exit. [44]

---

44. Sahih Al-Bukhari and Sahih Muslim

GOLDEN TICKET

DON'T MISS A DAILY GOLDEN OPPORTUNITY TO HAVE ALL YOUR DU'AAS ANSWERED

The Prophet *sallAllahu 'alayhi wa sallam* said, "Our Lord descends every night, during the last third of it, to the skies of this world and asks, 'Who is making du'aa to me so that I can respond to him? Who is asking me so that I can give him (his requests)? Who is asking for My forgiveness, so that I can forgive him?'"

Why Hasn't My *Du'aa* Been Answered Yet?

When a person makes a lot of *du'aa* for a long time, the *shaytaan* will come and whisper to make him give up. He or she may then fall into the mistake we mentioned earlier, wherein he says, *"I've made so much du'aa and it wasn't accepted!"* And this statement would then either prevent his *du'aa* from being accepted or make him give up on his *du'aa*.

But the question remains: why are some of our *du'aas* delayed? Why do some seem unanswered? Before we seek to answer these questions, we must remember that Allah is the *Rabb* and Owner of everything, so we should not doubt Him or have any bad thoughts regarding Him. Rather, we must always think and believe the best about Allah. The Prophet *sallAllahu 'alayhi wa sallam* informed us that Allah said, *"I am as my slave thinks of Me."* [45]

We know that Allah is the Most Merciful; we know that it's not because He wants to prevent good from coming to us or wants harm to come to us. And because He is the Most Powerful and able to do anything, we know that whatever we are asking is easy for Him. So the reason the *du'aa* is being delayed is because, in addition to being the Most Merciful, Generous, and Powerful, He is also the Most Knowledgeable and Most Wise. It is due to His limitless knowledge and wisdom that our *du'aas* may be delayed.

---

[45] Sahih Al-Bukhari and Sahih Muslim

WHY OUR *DU'AA* MAY BE DELAYED?

1 **P**erhaps having the request granted at a later time is in fact better than having it now, or having it now could actually be harmful.

2 **T**he thing you are asking for could be bad for you, so Allah will give you something better or remove a trial from you. And if you knew the result of having it, you would be relieved to know that Allah, due to His mercy and care for you, did not grant it to you.

3 **I**ts delay could simply be a test of your patience. Allah may be testing to see if you will maintain your strong belief in His Names and Attributes and trust that He knows and only chooses what is best for you because He is *Al-Mujeeb, Ar-Rahman*, etc.

4 **M**aybe your *du'aa* needs to be strengthened with some of the methods mentioned earlier to increase the chances of *du'aas* being accepted.

5 **T**he delay could be to increase your worship and your closeness to Allah, which is best for you. Perhaps this need is causing you to pray more mindfully, to feel more humility and need for Allah, to feel less self-sufficient and entitled, to make more *du'aa*, to know Allah's names more, and to do more acts of worship.

6 **M**aybe you need to make *tawbah* (repentance) from a sin or return the rights of someone so that your *du'aa* can be answered. For example, you took something from someone that did not belong to you, and they did not give it to you.. You must return that thing to the rightful owner first. The delay may be a great opportunity for self-reflection and growth and an opportunity to correct a wrongful act.

CHAPTER 3
REVIEW AND REFLECT QUESTIONS

1

Learning that Allah is *Al-Qareeb* (Most Near) and *Al-Mujeeb* (the One who responds), explain how these names of His help you feel closer to Him.

2

Perhaps you may have had times when you found yourself quickly mumbling a *du'aa* that you needed or wanted. After reading this section, describe how you feel your attitude towards making *du'aa* has changed and the actions you will take to ensure your *du'aas* are made under your best conditions and etiquettes possible.

3

Two hindrances that hold people back from making *du'aa* consistently are the fear of "asking for too much" and the frustration of their *du'aas* not being accepted. Explain to such a person why Allah loves that they make more *du'aa*, and the steps they can take to promote acceptance.

4

If someone extremely rich were to host you for a few days, wanting to treat you to as many things as possible, and then you restricted yourself to a few small requests, imagine how offended they would feel, not to mention how you would feel not making the most of what you could have had. Allah is capable of everything and does not get upset or humiliate you when you ask Him. How can making *du'aa* consistently upgrade your connection with Allah and benefit you in your life, capabilities, successes, and happiness?

5

Prophet Zakariyya *'alayhis salaam* mentioned Allah's favors to him before supplicating for a son and then explained the benefit of having a son for the next generations. What are some additional ways you can increase your *du'aas* in a similar manner?

CHAPTER 4

Al-Ghafoor, Al-Ghaffar, At-Tawwab
{The Most Forgiving}

ALLAH FORGIVES ME

Among the many qualities that fall under Allah's mercy are that He is *Al-Ghafoor*, *Al-Ghaffar* (the Most Forgiving), and *At-Tawwab* (the one who accepts repentance). *Al-Ghafoo*r and *Al-Ghaffar* both mean that Allah conceals the person's sins and pardons them.. *Al-Ghaffar* is the form of the word indicating that Allah continually forgives, time and time again.

Ta'ib (repentant) literally means someone who comes back. So a human is called *ta'ib* when he or she returns to Allah in repentance after doing wrong. *Tawwab* is a form of the same word, but it means someone who repents *constantly* - over and over again. In the case of Allah, *At-Tawwab* means He is always and constantly accepting His servants' repentance.

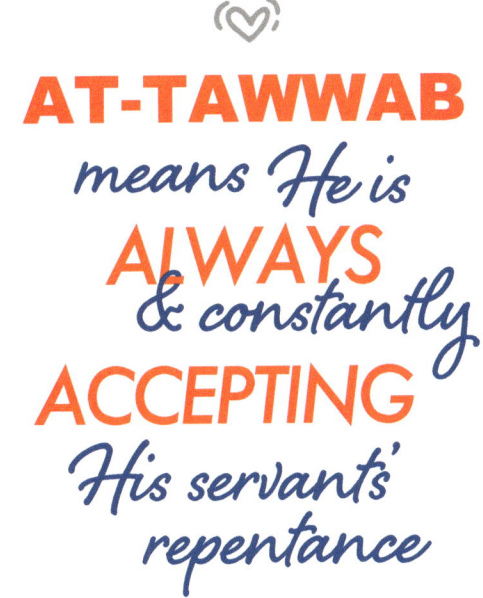

Journey to Allah Series **Who Is Allah?** | 49

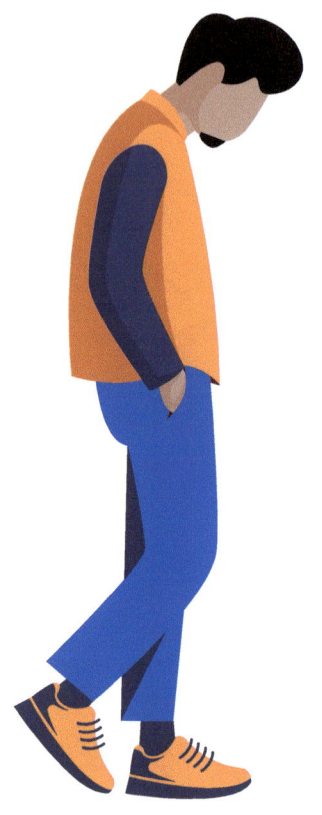

In other words, there is no upper limit on the magnitude of sins He will forgive or the number of times He forgives a person.

Furthermore, the name *At-Tawwab* includes two aspects: one appears even before the person's repentance and one after. Allah guides and inspires his servants to repent after sinning and facilitates the path of repentance for them. A person will find themselves filled with a feeling of regret and an urge to seek forgiveness. The conditions of repentance, which we will discuss shortly, will be made clear and possible for him or her. This is why Allah stated regarding three of the Prophet's companions who had committed a sin,

ثُمَّ تَابَ عَلَيْهِمْ لِيَتُوبُوا

"Then He turned to them in tawbah so that they may turn to him (in) tawbah." *

In other words, Allah knew that they were sincere but erred as all humans do, so He inspired their hearts to sincerely repent. The second aspect of *tawbah* is that after the person repents, Allah forgives him or her and erases the sin and its consequences in both this life and the next, as if it never even took place.

"AND WHOEVER COMMITS A WRONGDOING OR WRONGS HIMSELF BUT THEN SEEKS ALLAH'S FORGIVENESS WILL FIND ALLAH MOST FORGIVING, MOST MERCIFUL."

The Prophet *sallAllahu 'alayhi wa sallam* also explained, *"The person who has repented from a sin is just like the person who has no sin (to begin with)."* [46]

---

* Surah At-Tawbah [9:118]
46. Ibn Majah

Journey to Allah Series *Who Is Allah?* | 50

Allah Invites Us to Repent-Time and Time Again

From His immense mercy, Allah calls on us to come back to Him in repentance. Here are just a few examples mentioned in the *Qur'an*.

وَهُوَ ٱلَّذِى يَقْبَلُ ٱلتَّوْبَةَ عَنْ عِبَادِهِ وَيَعْفُوا عَنِ ٱلسَّيِّئَاتِ

"And He is the one who accepts the repentance from His servants and forgives their sins..." [47]

أَلَمْ يَعْلَمُوا أَنَّ ٱللَّهَ هُوَ يَقْبَلُ ٱلتَّوْبَةَ عَنْ عِبَادِهِ وَيَأْخُذُ ٱلصَّدَقَٰتِ وَأَنَّ ٱللَّهَ هُوَ ٱلتَّوَّابُ ٱلرَّحِيمُ

"Don't they know that Allah is the One who accepts the repentance of His servants and accepts their charity, and that Allah is the one who is At-Tawwab, Ar-Raheem?" [48]

أَفَلَا يَتُوبُونَ إِلَى ٱللَّهِ وَيَسْتَغْفِرُونَهُ وَٱللَّهُ غَفُورٌ رَّحِيمٌ

"Will they not, then, repent to Allah and ask His forgiveness? For, He is the Most Forgiving, the Most Merciful." [49]

The Prophet *sallAllahu 'alayhi wa sallam* said that Allah says, *"O my servants! You indeed commit wrong in the night and in the day, and I forgive all sins; so seek my forgiveness, and I will forgive you."* [50]

Allah Loves For Us to Do Tawbah (Repentance)

Not only does He call on us to repent, He encourages us by explaining to us how much He loves our repentance. He said, *"Indeed Allah loves those who continually repent and those who purify themselves."* [51]

He also informed us that the angels carrying His throne will pray for those who repent to Allah:

ٱلَّذِينَ يَحْمِلُونَ ٱلْعَرْشَ وَمَنْ حَوْلَهُ يُسَبِّحُونَ بِحَمْدِ رَبِّهِمْ وَيُؤْمِنُونَ بِهِ وَيَسْتَغْفِرُونَ لِلَّذِينَ ءَامَنُوا رَبَّنَا وَسِعْتَ كُلَّ شَىْءٍ رَّحْمَةً وَعِلْمًا فَٱغْفِرْ لِلَّذِينَ تَابُوا وَٱتَّبَعُوا سَبِيلَكَ وَقِهِمْ عَذَابَ ٱلْجَحِيمِ

"Those (angels) carrying the throne, as well as this around them, exalt their Lord's praises and believe in Him. And they seek forgiveness for the believers (saying), 'Our Rabb, you have encompassed everything with mercy and knowledge, so forgive those who make tawbah and follow your path; and save them from the punishment of the Fire.'" [52]

---

47. Surah Ash-Shuraa [42:25]
48. Surah At-Tawbah [9:104]
49. Surah Al-Ma'idah [5:74]
50. Sahih Muslim
51. Surah Al-Baqarah [2:222]
52. Surah Ghaafir [40:7]

Allah Forgives All Sins, No Matter How Great

No matter how serious or major a sin was, no matter how many times a person has committed it, once he or she repents sincerely, Allah will forgive it completely. Allah tells us,

قُلْ يَـٰعِبَادِىَ ٱلَّذِينَ أَسْرَفُوا۟ عَلَىٰٓ أَنفُسِهِمْ لَا تَقْنَطُوا۟ مِن رَّحْمَةِ ٱللَّهِ إِنَّ ٱللَّهَ يَغْفِرُ ٱلذُّنُوبَ جَمِيعًا إِنَّهُ هُوَ ٱلْغَفُورُ ٱلرَّحِيمُ

"Say, 'O My servants who have wronged themselves (by excessively sinning), do not despair of the mercy of Allah. Indeed, Allah forgives all sins. Indeed, it is He who is the Forgiving, the Merciful.'" 53

Our scholars explained that this ayah means that Allah forgives all sins if the person sincerely repents.

Allah also declares,

إِلَّا مَن تَابَ وَءَامَنَ وَعَمِلَ عَمَلًا صَـٰلِحًا فَأُو۟لَـٰٓئِكَ يُبَدِّلُ ٱللَّهُ سَيِّـَٔاتِهِمْ حَسَنَـٰتٍ وَكَانَ ٱللَّهُ غَفُورًا رَّحِيمًا وَمَن تَابَ وَعَمِلَ صَـٰلِحًا فَإِنَّهُۥ يَتُوبُ إِلَى ٱللَّهِ مَتَابًا

"Except for those who repent (from these sins), believe, and do righteous deeds. For them, Allah will replace their evil deeds with good. And ever is Allah Forgiving and Merciful. And he who repents and does righteousness does indeed turn to Allah with [accepted] repentance." 54

After mentioning the most major of sins, Allah tells us that not only will He completely forgive those who repent from these major sins, but He will replace their evil deeds with good deeds!

---

53. Surah Az-Zumar [39:53]
54. Surah Al-Furqaan [25:70-71]

HE WAS FORGIVEN

To emphasize that no sin is too great for Allah to forgive for one who repents, the Prophet sallAllahu 'alayhi wa sallam told us this true story, which occurred in one of the nations of the previous prophets.

There was a person before you who had killed ninety-nine people; then he asked about the most knowledgeable person (in religion) in the world (who could show him the way to salvation). He was directed to a monk. He came to him and told him that he had killed ninety-nine people and asked him whether there was any way that his repentance would be accepted. He replied, "No!" So he killed him too, thereby killing one hundred people. He again asked about the most knowledgeable person in the world and was directed to a religious scholar. He told him that he had killed a hundred people and asked him whether there was any possible way for his repentance to be accepted. He said: "Yes; what could possibly stand between you and repentance? Go to such and such a land; there are people there devoted to prayer and worship, so go worship (Allah) along with them. And do not return to your (home) because it is a place of evil (for you)."

So he went away and reached half the distance when death came to him. Then the angels of mercy and the angels of punishment began disputing. The angels of mercy said, "This man has come as a repentant person, trying to come closer to Allah!" But the angels of punishment replied, "But he has not done a single good deed!" Then came another angel in the form of a human being in order to judge the matter between them. He said, "Measure which land he is closer to and decide accordingly." They measured it and found him nearer to the land where he intended to go (the land of piety), and so the angels of mercy took him.

Another narration states, "Allah commanded (the land that he wanted to leave) to move away and commanded the other land (his destination) to draw nearer, and then He said: 'Now measure the distance between them.' It was found that he was nearer to his goal by a hand's span and was thus forgiven." [56]

---

56. Sahih Muslim

This *hadith* shows us that we should never feel hopeless of Allah's forgiveness if we repent, nor should we cause others who have done wrong to feel hopeless. The repentant person may end up more beloved to Allah than the one who did not repent, depending on his or her state afterwards. Furthermore, we learn from this *hadith* that if a person commits the same sin chronically or the sin is of an addictive nature, he or she should try to determine the factors and environment that lead to the sin and change them in order for a real change to take place. For example, we may need to change our circle of friends, our Internet habits, or other factors in our environment.

HOW TO SINCERELY REPENT

REGRET

Feeling bad in your heart about the wrong you have done.

RESOLVE

Determination never to repeat that.

REMOVE

In order to stop the sin, you need to remove yourself from the situation that causes you to sin.

REDRESS

If the sin involves taking other people's rights that need to be returned.

THE 4 'R'S OF REPENTANCE

1 REGRET

The reason anyone would want to repent is because they feel badly about the wrong they've done.

2 REMOVE

Removing yourself from the situation that causes you to sin will help you from sinning. For example, if you are trying to stay away from backbiting, then refrain from attending gatherings where people tend to gossip. This means that at the time we decide to repent, we should stop engaging in the sin. A person cannot truly repent and continue committing the sin at the same time. The way to stop sinning is to remove oneself from the situation that leads to sin.

3 RESOLVE

Determination to never repeat it. We should be determined not to repeat the wrong and try to change whatever factors lead to it, as we mentioned earlier. However, if a person sincerely repents and genuinely resolves not to repeat the sin but later happens to weaken and fall into the sin again, the first repentance is still accepted, and he or she needs to repent sincerely again.

4 REDRESS

If the sin encompassed taking other people's rights, those rights must be returned. For example, if a person steals, he or she must return what was stolen. If a person slanders someone else (by telling lies about him or her), he or she must go back to the people they told the lies to and tell them that it was not true and that they were wrong.

I'm Trying But I Keep Making Mistakes!

> **NEWSFLASH!**
>
> We're humans, and we can't change that! What we can change is our response to those mistakes and how we learn and grow from them. The Prophet sallAllahu 'alayhi wa sallam assured us of this, saying, *"Every human being continuously makes mistakes, and the best of those who continually make mistakes are those who continually repent."* [57]

He sallAllahu 'alayhi wa sallam said, *"If someone commits a sin and then says, 'O my Lord! I have sinned; please forgive me!' His Lord responds, 'My servant knows that he has a Lord who forgives sins and punishes for them, so I have forgiven my servant.' Then he remains without committing any sin for a while until again he commits another sin and says, 'O my Lord, I have committed another sin; please forgive me!' Allah responds, 'My slave realized that he has a Lord who forgives sins and punishes for them, so I have forgiven my slave (his sin). Then he remains without committing any other sin for a while, but then falls into another sin and says, 'O my Lord, I have committed another sin; please forgive me.' Allah says, 'My slave has known that he has a Lord Who forgives sins and punishes for it, so I have forgiven My slave (his sin); he can do whatever he wishes."* [58]

He further clarified this concept by explaining that a sincere Muslim makes mistakes and feels regretful because he believes that Allah will hold him to account, so he sincerely repents because he also believes in Allah's promise to forgive the repentant. Allah sees that the person consistently repents and will continue to do so for the rest of his life, so He announces that He has already forgiven him!

---

57. At-Tirmidhi, Ahmad
58. Sahih Al-Bukhari and Sahih Muslim

Attitude:

"Oh It's Not a Big Deal! Allah is Most Forgiving!"

As we have learned in the previous *hadiths*, Allah forgives those who **sincerely** repent. That is, a person falls into a sin out of human weakness, then sincerely feels bad about it and fears the consequences of what he/she has done and seeks Allah's forgiveness, making the necessary changes that will prevent them from falling into the sin again. Allah is Most Merciful and Most Forgiving to such people. However, He also knows what is in our hearts, so we cannot plan to sin with the excuse that we will make *tawbah* after. Nor should His mercy lead us to commit more sins under the excuse that He is Most Merciful! Rather, the more sincere a person is, the closer he or she tries to come to Allah, the more good deeds he or she does and sins he or she avoids, and the more deserving he or she will be of Allah's special *rahmah*. For example, Allah says,

إِنَّ ٱلَّذِينَ ءَامَنُوا وَٱلَّذِينَ هَاجَرُوا وَجَٰهَدُوا فِى سَبِيلِ ٱللَّهِ أُو۟لَٰٓئِكَ يَرْجُونَ رَحْمَتَ ٱللَّهِ وَٱللَّهُ غَفُورٌ رَّحِيمٌ

"Indeed, those who believe and those who emigrate and fight in the way of Allah,, they are the ones who hope for Allah's mercy. And Allah is the Most Forgiving, Most Merciful." [59]

---

59. Surah Al-Baqarah [2:218]

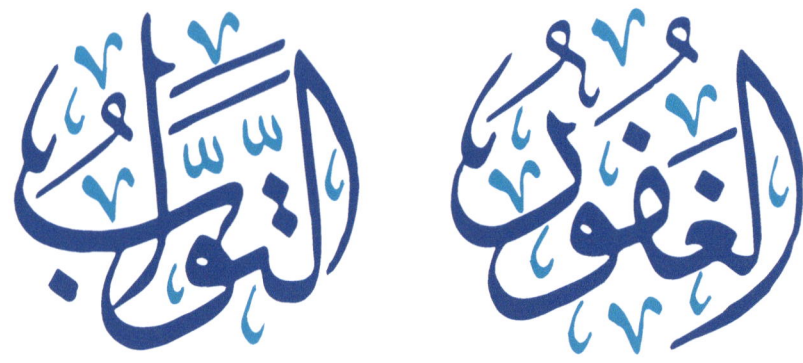

What does having *tawheed* in *At-Tawwab* and *Al-Ghafoor* mean?

Believing that Allah is One and Unique in this beautiful attribute encompasses belief in the following:

- No one besides Allah can guide people to repent.

- No one except Him can erase sins.

- No one except Him forgives the sins and conceals them.

- Human forgiveness is imperfect and incomplete, while Allah is the **only One** (*tawheed*) with perfect and complete forgiveness. If you keep making mistakes over and over again, which human will continually forgive you? Even if they do forgive you, will they act like it never happened over and over (and over) again? As humans, we hold grudges, we have a limit on how much we can forgive others before considering it too much, we talk to others about the wrongs that have been done to us, we may forgive some people and not others. Our forgiveness may be based on the magnitude of the wrong, and so on. But Allah's forgiveness isn't.

THE EFFECTS OF "AT-TAWWAB" ON ME

1

It increases my love of Allah and attachment to Him above all others. After all, He is the only one who can erase sins. He forgives in a way no human ever could!

2

It increases my desire to come closer to Him because His mercy is so encompassing.

3

It increases my hope in Him and prevents me from falling into despair when I do commit a sin. Rather, I will use my sin as an opportunity to worship Him by the names *At-Tawwab* and, *Al-Ghafoor* by making sincere *tawbah*, recalling the *ayaat* and *hadiths*, and believing in them with full conviction.

4

It will lead me to make *tawbah* as soon as I make a mistake and try to follow it up with good deeds.

5

I will make a lot of *istighfaar* for the sins I know and don't know.

6

I will leave bad company and corrupt environments and situations that lead me to sins because one of the conditions of *tawbah* is to be determined to not repeat it.

7

It will cause me to do more good deeds in general, knowing that they will wipe out my bad deeds. The Prophet *sallAllahu 'alayhi wa sallam* said, *"Follow up your bad deed with a good one, and it will erase it."* [60]

8

I will avoid sins to the best of my ability because I am ashamed and don't want to anger Allah.

9

I will forgive others, so Allah will forgive me.

---

60. At-Tirmidhi

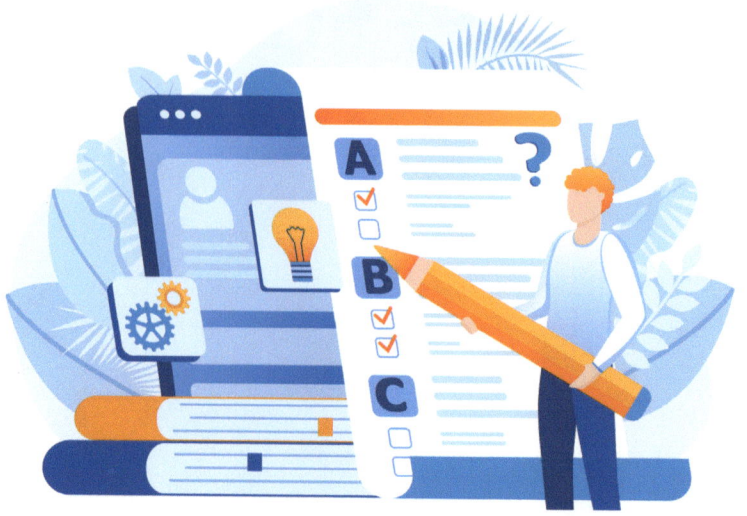

CHAPTER 4

REVIEW AND REFLECT QUESTIONS

1

We learned from this section that changing your surroundings can help curb your bad habits. Why is it important to surround yourself with righteous people or be in a righteous community? What do you feel are the benefits in this life and the hereafter for doing so?

2

There are two aspects of *tawbah*, one before a person repents and then the forgiveness that is given after their repentance. How does knowing more about Allah's mercy and his willingness to forgive increase a person's urge to seek forgiveness?

3

A vital step in sincere repentance is resolve. What can resolve look like?

4

How has your concept of repentance changed after reading this section? Did you ever consider repentance as an act of worship?

5

A part of being human is making mistakes. Imagine your friend coming up to you and declaring he is such a bad person because of all the sins he keeps falling into. What advice would you give him to help him understand that the door of repentance is always open?

CHAPTER 5

Ash-Shakoor
{The Most Appreciative}

ALLAH APPRECIATES ME

Allah says in the *Qur'an*,

إِنَّهُ غَفُورٌ شَكُورٌ

"Truly, He is Al-Ghafoor (Most Forgiving), Ash-Shakoor (Most Appreciative)." [61]

فَإِنَّ ٱللَّهَ شَاكِرٌ عَلِيمٌ

"Indeed Allah is Shakir, All-Knowing." [62]

Shukr means gratitude for and appreciation of the good others do. So a grateful (*shakoor*) servant of Allah is one who recognizes that the blessings are from Allah, feels grateful for it, and thanks Him for it. But what does it mean with regards to Allah? Allah is the Most Appreciative and *"thanks"* His servants' good deeds. But in the case of Allah, our good does not benefit Him; it's for our own good!

Al-Shakoor HE IS THE MOST APPRECIATIVE & "Thanks" HIS SERVANTS' good deeds.

---

61. Surah Fatir [35:30]
62. Surah Al-Baqarah [2:158]

How Exactly is Allah Ash-Shakoor?

With regards to Allah, being the Most Appreciative means many things, all of which show that He leaves nothing unappreciated and unrewarded.

1 REWARDING GOOD ACTS

Allah is pleased with, appreciates, and rewards even the slightest good that His servants do sincerely for His sake. No good deed, no matter how small or insignificant it may seem, goes unnoticed or unappreciated.

For example, the Prophet sallAllahu 'alayhi wa sallam said, "While a man was on his way (somewhere), he felt very thirsty and came across a well. He climbed down, quenched his thirst, and came out. He then saw a dog panting and licking mud out of his extreme thirst. He said to himself, 'This dog is suffering from extreme thirst just as I did.' So he went down the well again and filled his shoe with water and gave it (to the dog) to drink. Allah thanked him for that deed and forgave him." The companions (who heard this) said, "O Allah's Messenger sallAllahu 'alayhi wa sallam! Do we get rewarded for being kind to animals?" He replied: "Yes, there is a reward for serving any living thing." [63]

The Messenger of Allah sallAllahu 'alayhi wa sallam also narrated to us the following story: "Once a prostitute from Bani Israel saw a thirsty dog going around and around a well, on the verge of dying from thirst. So she filled her shoe with water and let him drink it. So Allah forgave her sins because of that good deed." [64] Our scholars explained that this was because of her sincerity and compassion.

He sallAllahu 'alayhi wa sallam also said, "As a man was walking on a path, he saw a thorny branch, so he removed it. Allah thanked him for this deed by forgiving him." [65]

ACTIVITY

Write down two things that you did today that were selfless and two things that were selfish.

---

63. Sahih Muslim
64. Sahih Al-Bukhari and Sahih Muslim
65. Sahih Al-Bukhari and Sahih Muslim

2 | MULTIPLYING REWARD

Allah shows His appreciation for a good deed by multiplying and magnifying its reward but doesn't do the same for the sin. Allah explains this saying,

مَن جَاءَ بِالْحَسَنَةِ فَلَهُ عَشْرُ أَمْثَالِهَا وَمَن جَاءَ بِالسَّيِّئَةِ فَلَا يُجْزَىٰ إِلَّا مِثْلَهَا وَهُمْ لَا يُظْلَمُونَ

"Whoever comes with a good deed will have ten times the like thereof, and whoever comes with an evil deed will not be recompensed except the like thereof; and they will not be wronged." 66

The Prophet *sallAllahu 'alayhi wa sallam* said, *"Indeed Allah wrote the good and evil deeds then made them clear. So whoever intends to do a good deed but does not do it, Allah will record it as a complete good deed for him. But whoever intends it and actually does it, Allah, the Most Glorious and Exalted, will record it multiplied by ten to seven hundred times, or even greater. On the other hand, whoever intends to do wrong but refrains from doing it, Allah will record this as a good deed. And if he intends it and actually does it, it will be written as one sin."* 67

3 | REWARDING GOOD INTENTIONS

Allah appreciates and rewards a good intention, even if the person didn't act on it.

If a person intends to perform the night prayer (*qiyam al-layl*) but oversleeps, Allah will reward him as if he prayed it. The Prophet *sallAllahu 'alayhi wa sallam* explained, *"Whoever goes to bed intending to wake up and pray (qiyam) during the night but is overwhelmed by sleep until the morning, what he intended (the qiyam) will be recorded for him, and his sleep is a charity given to him by his Lord."* 68

---

66. Surah Al-An'aam [6:160]
67. Sahih Al-Bukhari and Sahih Muslim
68. Abu Dawood, An-Nasaa'ee, Musnad Ahmad

4 REMEMBERING ALLAH

Allah appreciates our remembrance of Him, whether simply within ourselves or stated verbally in solitude or to other people.

The Prophet sallAllahu 'alayhi wa sallam said, "Allah says: 'I am just as My slave thinks of me. And I am with him if He remembers Me. If he remembers Me in himself, I too remember him in Myself; and if he remembers Me in a group of people, I remember him in a group that is better than they; and if he comes one span nearer to Me, I go one cubit nearer to him; and if he comes one cubit nearer to Me, I go a distance of two outstretched arms nearer to him; and if he comes to Me walking, I go to him running." [69]

5 SACRIFICING

When someone leaves something for His sake, He appreciates it by giving him something better.

The Prophet sallAllahu 'alayhi wa sallam said, "Indeed, you will never leave something for the sake of Allah except that He will replace it with something better for you." [70]

Allah made this clear in the story of Prophet Ibrahim 'alayhis salaam. Ibrahim 'alayhis salaam left his family, his community, and his home when his people persisted in idolatry. Undoubtedly, this is a difficult sacrifice. Allah appreciated this huge sacrifice and granted Ibrahim instead a beautiful, righteous family and made his children not only righteous but prophets as well! Allah explains,

فَلَمَّا ٱعْتَزَلَهُمْ وَمَا يَعْبُدُونَ مِن دُونِ ٱللَّهِ وَهَبْنَا لَهُۥٓ إِسْحَٰقَ وَيَعْقُوبَ وَكُلًّا جَعَلْنَا نَبِيًّا

"So when He removed himself away from them and what they worship besides Allah, We granted him Ishaq and Yaqoob and made all of them prophets." [71]

---

69. Sahih Al-Bukhari and Sahih Muslim
70. Ahmad
71. Surah Maryam [19:49]

Similarly, if someone leaves bad friends for Allah, Allah will appreciate such a sacrifice and *"thank"* the person by granting them righteous companions who will be even more beloved to him or her. If a person leaves a job opportunity because it requires him or her to compromise their *deen* (religion), Allah will grant them better.

6 | BEARING HARDSHIPS

Allah appreciates any struggle or suffering a person undergoes for His sake by replacing it with something greater.

When the *sahabah* fled their homes for His sake, He rewarded them by making them the just rulers of huge portions of the whole world. When Yusuf *'alayhi wa salaam* patiently bore his life in prison, trusting in and accepting Allah's decree, Allah *"thanked"* him by giving him authority over all of Egypt.

Similarly, the Prophet *sallAllahu 'alayhi wa sallam* said, *"Sadaqah will not decrease a person's money. Allah will only increase the one who forgives with honor and dignity. And no one humbles himself for the sake of Allah except that Allah will elevate his status."* [72]

---

72. Sahih Muslim

Effects of Ash-Shakoor on me

I WILL ONLY SEEK ALLAH'S APPRECIATION:
I will not seek people's gratitude and appreciation, but Allah's, even when I am doing good to others. As such, I will not feel disappointed or upset if they do not show me gratitude or appreciation. It will be enough for me that Allah appreciates and rewards it.

I AM MOTIVATED TO DO GOOD DEEDS
It will encourage me to do more good deeds because I know that each one will be multiplied. I will do my deeds while consciously bearing in mind the great reward and Allah's appreciation of this deed.

MY LOVE FOR ALLAH INCREASES

I WILL BE GRATEFUL AND THANKFUL:
I will be a thankful, grateful slave of Allah because Allah loves gratitude and appreciation. If Allah grants me a blessing, I will show gratitude with my heart by recognizing that it is from Allah and not my own self or others. I will thank Allah by saying, *"Alhamdulillah"* for the blessing. And I will thank Him with my actions by using the blessing in a way that pleases Allah.

I PURIFY MY INTENTION
I will make sure I have a righteous intention when doing any action, no matter how small it may be. This way I will be rewarded if I am unable to do it. And if I am able to, its reward will be multiplied if I do.

I WILL REFRAIN FROM COMMITTING A SIN
If I am tempted to do wrong or consider committing a sin, I will refrain myself, remembering how much Allah will appreciate it and write it as a good deed.

I WILL APPRECIATE OTHERS FOR THEIR KINDNESS:
Because Allah loves the quality of gratitude, I will show appreciation to other people.

EVERY GOOD DEED IS IMPORTANT TO ME:
I will not belittle any good or small acts of kindness.

Allah says, أَنِ اشْكُرْ لِي وَلِوَالِدَيْكَ
"... So thank me and your parents..." [73] The Prophet *sallAllahu 'alayhi wa sallam* said, *"Whoever does not thank the people has not thanked Allah."* [74]

---

73. Surah Luqman [31:14]
74. At-Tirmidhi

CHAPTER 5
REVIEW AND REFLECT QUESTIONS

1

"The most beloved of deeds to Allah are those that are consistent, even if it is small." [75] Keeping this *hadith* in mind, how should our attitude be towards making small sacrifices for the sake of Allah first? What are some small sacrifices that you can make in your daily life to be a better Muslim.

2

Allah is very Merciful to his servants; just by having a good intention, you will get a reward, even if you did not act upon it. Let us examine two girls and how they start their days. The first girl writes down ten good deeds that she wants to complete for the day and the second girl goes throughout her day doing good deeds as they come along. Who do you think may benefit more, and why?

3

Many Muslims stop performing good deeds because they say their intention is not pure. What advice would you give to a person who feels that way? Should we stop doing good deeds because our intentions aren't pure?

4

Showing gratitude to Allah can be as simple as just thanking Him for the blessings He has given to you. Can you think of three other ways that you can display your gratitude to Allah from the *Qur'an* or *hadith* that you know?

---

75. Sahih Al-Bukhari

BRAIN TEASER

How many Names and Attributes of Allah can you find in the following *ayaat*?

هُوَ ٱللَّهُ ٱلَّذِى لَآ إِلَـٰهَ إِلَّا هُوَ ۖ عَـٰلِمُ ٱلْغَيْبِ وَٱلشَّهَـٰدَةِ ۖ هُوَ ٱلرَّحْمَـٰنُ ٱلرَّحِيمُ ۚ

هُوَ ٱللَّهُ ٱلَّذِى لَآ إِلَـٰهَ إِلَّا هُوَ ٱلْمَلِكُ ٱلْقُدُّوسُ ٱلسَّلَـٰمُ ٱلْمُؤْمِنُ ٱلْمُهَيْمِنُ ٱلْعَزِيزُ ٱلْجَبَّارُ ٱلْمُتَكَبِّرُ ۚ سُبْحَـٰنَ ٱللَّهِ عَمَّا يُشْرِكُونَ ۚ

هُوَ ٱللَّهُ ٱلْخَـٰلِقُ ٱلْبَارِئُ ٱلْمُصَوِّرُ ۖ لَهُ ٱلْأَسْمَآءُ ٱلْحُسْنَىٰ ۚ يُسَبِّحُ لَهُۥ مَا فِى ٱلسَّمَـٰوَٰتِ وَٱلْأَرْضِ ۖ وَهُوَ ٱلْعَزِيزُ ٱلْحَكِيمُ ۚ

CHAPTER 6

Al- Wadood

{ The Most Loving }

ALLAH LOVES ME

Allah says,

وَٱسْتَغْفِرُوا رَبَّكُمْ ثُمَّ تُوبُوٓا إِلَيْهِ إِنَّ رَبِّى رَحِيمٌ وَدُودٌ

"And ask your Lord for forgiveness, then repent to Him. Truly, my Lord is Raheem (Most Merciful), Wadood (Most Loving for)." [76]

He also said,

وَهُوَ ٱلْغَفُورُ ٱلْوَدُودُ

"And He is Al-Ghafoor (the Most Forgiving), Al-Wadood (the Most Loving)." [77]

The scholars said that *Al-Wadood* means both that He is Most Loving and loved by creation.

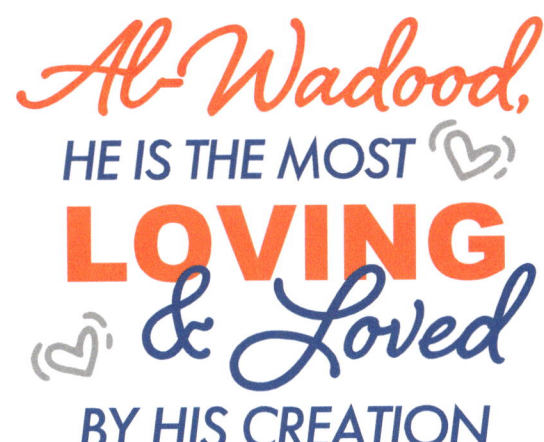

Al-Wadood, HE IS THE MOST LOVING & Loved BY HIS CREATION

---

76. Surah Hud [11:90]
77. Surah Al-Buruj [85:14]

What Happens When Allah Loves Someone?

The Prophet *sallAllahu 'alayhi wa sallam* stated that Allah says:

"Whoever shows enmity to a close servant (Wali) of Mine, I will declare war on him. My servant draws near to Me with nothing more beloved to Me than the obligations I have instructed him with. My servant continues to draw closer to Me with voluntary good deeds until I love him. And when I love him, I become his hearing with which he hears, his sight with which he sees, his hand with which he strikes, and his foot with which he walks. And if he were to ask anything of Me, I would surely give it to him; and if he were to ask Me for refuge, I would surely grant it to him. I do not hesitate to [do] anything as much as I hesitate to [seize] the soul of My believing servant, for he hates death, and I hate hurting him." [78]

---

78. Sahih Al-Bukhari

Oftentimes, we engage in actions that Allah does not love for the sake of attaining other people's love, attention, affection, or approval, while in fact, we forget that even people's love and acceptance are in the hands of Allah! Haven't you ever met someone whom everyone seems to love and respect? When Allah loves someone, He inspires all of creation to love them. Allah says,

إِنَّ ٱلَّذِينَ ءَامَنُوا وَعَمِلُوا ٱلصَّٰلِحَٰتِ سَيَجْعَلُ لَهُمُ ٱلرَّحْمَٰنُ وُدًّا

"Indeed, those who believe and do righteous deeds, the Most Merciful will grant them a love (from Himself and from others)." [79]

Furthermore, Allah's Messenger *sallAllahu 'alayhi wa sallam* said, *"If Allah loves a person, He calls (Angel) Jibreel, saying, 'Allah loves so and so, O Jibreel, so love him.' So Jibreel then loves him and announces in the Heavens (to the other angels): 'Allah loves so and-so, so you should also love him.' So all the inhabitants of the Heavens love him. and then the people on earth are also (caused to) love him."* [80]

How Can I Attain Allah's Love?

1

Repentance. Attaining Allah's love does not mean that you will never sin or do wrong. Rather, Allah loves repentance and those who repent whenever they fall into any sin, no matter how major or minor. What is the evidence for this? Allah connected His attribute of being the Most Loving to the act of asking His forgiveness.

وَٱسْتَغْفِرُوا رَبَّكُمْ ثُمَّ تُوبُوٓا إِلَيْهِ إِنَّ رَبِّى رَحِيمٌ وَدُودٌ

"And ask your Lord for forgiveness, then repent to Him. Truly, my Lord is Most Merciful, **Most Loving***."* [81]

Allah also says,

إِنَّ ٱللَّهَ يُحِبُّ ٱلتَّوَّٰبِينَ وَيُحِبُّ ٱلْمُتَطَهِّرِينَ

"Truly, **Allah loves those who constantly repent** *and purify themselves."* [82]

2

Think about and long for the meeting with Allah. The Prophet *sallAllahu 'alayhi wa sallam* said, *"He who loves meeting Allah, Allah loves to meet him."* [83] How can we love our meeting with Allah? Read about the Day of Judgment and the people of Paradise and imagine... Imagine how beautiful it will be to finally hear Allah and see Him directly. Imagine how relieving it would be to hear Allah inform you that He forgave all your sins. Imagine how beautiful it would be to hear

---

79. Surah Maryam [19:96]
80. Sahih Muslim
81. Surah Hud [11:90]
82. Surah Al-Baqarah [2:222]
83. Sahih Muslim

Him say,

$$ادْخُلُوهَا بِسَلَٰمٍ ءَامِنِينَ$$

"Enter my Paradise in peace and security." [84] Imagine yourself in *Jannah*, and He asks you, *"Is there anything else you wish for me to give you?"* [85]

3

Learn about the Prophet *sallAllahu 'alayhi wa sallam*, which will naturally cause you to love him, then follow his example. Allah says,

$$قُلْ إِن كُنتُمْ تُحِبُّونَ ٱللَّهَ فَٱتَّبِعُونِى يُحْبِبْكُمُ ٱللَّهُ وَيَغْفِرْ لَكُمْ ذُنُوبَكُمْ وَٱللَّهُ غَفُورٌ رَّحِيمٌ$$

"Say, (O Prophet), "If you love Allah, then follow me; Allah will love you and forgive your sins. For Allah is All-Forgiving, Most Merciful." [86]

4

Establish your Islamic obligations first. This is based on the above-mentioned *hadith*, wherein Allah says, *"My servant draws near to Me with **nothing more beloved to Me** than the obligations I have enjoined upon him."* [87] For example, make sure your prayers are done properly, on time, and with concentration. Be good to your parents for the sake of Allah. Ensure you are wearing the proper hijab as He instructed. And part of doing what Allah has made obligatory is avoiding the *haram* (the forbidden actions). Do not lie, cheat, steal, curse, harm others, and so on. Protect your eyes from looking at, hearing, or touching anything sinful.

5

After your obligations are established, perform voluntary acts of worship consistently. This is also based on the continuation of the above *hadith*, in which Allah says, *"My servant continues to draw near to Me with voluntary deeds until I love him."* [88]

The goal is to choose recommended deeds that you can steadily maintain, even if they are small in nature. The Prophet *sallAllahu 'alayhi wa sallam* said, *"The most beloved deeds to Allah are the most consistent, even if they are small."* [89] For example, give regular charity, pray some *sunnah* prayers, recite a consistent amount of *Qur'an* daily, and establish some voluntary fasts.

6

Love the *Qur'an* and recite what you love. If we want to love Allah and want Him to love us, we would love His words and love hearing what He has to say. We would love hearing Him describe Himself, His actions, His attributes, His wisdom, His advice, His stories - everything He has to say. There was once a companion of the Prophet *sallAllahu 'alayhi wa sallam* who always ended his recitation in prayer with Surah Al-Ikhlaas. When the companions told the Prophet *sallAllahu 'alayhi wa sallam* this, he said, *"Ask him why he does that."* The man responded, *"Because it contains a description of Ar-Rahman, so I love to recite it."* The Prophet *sallAllahu 'alayhi wa sallam* said, *"Inform him that Allah loves him."* It wasn't simply for reciting Surah Al-Ikhlaas; it was also because he loved doing so and loved what it contained! This shows us Allah's love for the quality of the deed rather than the quantity.

---

84. Surah Al-Hijr [15:46]
85. Sahih Muslim

7

Love others for the sake of Allah and fulfill their rights. This means loving those who love, obey, and strive to please Allah, and loving those who remind, encourage, and motivate us to come closer to Him. The Prophet *sallAllahu 'alayhi wa sallam* said that Allah says, *"My love is obligatory for those who love each other for My Sake, those who sit with one another for My Sake, those who visit each other for My Sake, and those who spend on one another for My Sake."* [90]

8

Strengthen your *iman*, your character, and your body. Signs of a strong character include not compromising your religion for the sake of others, speaking out against wrong, defending the truth, being proud of your identity as a practicing Muslim, and doing what is right before Allah even when those around you are not. The Prophet *sallAllahu 'alayhi wa sallam* said, "The strong believer is better and more beloved to Allah than the weak believers, although both are good." [91]

9

Be truthful, trustworthy, and a good neighbor. The Prophet *sallAllahu 'alayhi wa sallam* said, "Whoever would be pleased to love Allah and His Messenger, or be loved by Allah and his Messenger, should be truthful whenever he speaks, protect any trust he is entrusted with, and be good to whomever he neighbors." [92]

10

Give preference to what Allah loves over what you love. Consider the following *hadith* and ask yourself what these three people's actions had in common. The Prophet *sallAllahu 'alayhi wa sallam* said, "(The following) three people, Allah will love, laughs to, [93] and rejoice at: A man (in battle) and his group fled. So He fights the enemy alone such that he will either be killed or Allah will grant him victory and suffice him. So Allah will say, 'Look at My servant, how he made himself patient for Me.' The one who has a beautiful wife (spouse) and comfortable bed, so he gets up at night to pray. Allah says, 'He left his desires to remember Me and call on Me in private. And had he wished, he could have slept.' A person who journeys with a group. They stay up late, become exhausted, then finally sleep. Meanwhile, he gets up before Fajr (to pray the night prayer), regardless of whether he is in ease or hardship." [94]

---

86. Surah Ale-'Imraan [3:31]
87. Sahih Al-Bukhari
88. Ibid.
89. Sahih Al-Bukhari and Sahih Muslim
90. Ahmad, Malik
91. Sahih Muslim
92. At-Tabarani
93. What does it mean that Allah laughs to a person? The Prophet *sallAllahu 'alayhi wa sallam* said, "If Allah laughs to a person, then (the person) will have no account on the Day of Judgment ." (Musnad Ahmad)
94. Al-Hakim, Al-Bayhaqi

ATTAINING ALLAH'S LOVE BY...

1. REPENTING

2. LEARNING ABOUT THE PROPHET *SALLALLAHU 'ALAYHI WA SALLAM.*

3. ALWAYS BEING TRUTHFUL

4. STRENGHTHENING YOUR IMAAN

5. LONGING TO MEET ALLAH

6. CONSISTENT VOLUNTARY ACTS

7. PRACTICING ISLAM

8. LOVING OTHERS FOR ALLAH'S SAKE

9. LOVING & RECITING THE *QUR'AN*

10. CHOOSING WHAT ALLAH LOVES

How to Increase Our Love of Allah?

1. Learn about Allah by studying the meanings of His Names and Attributes (as we are doing in this section).

2. Reflect on His Names and Attributes in each situation. Ask yourself, in this situation, which names of Allah do I see manifesting?

3. Spend time communicating with Allah. How? When we recite the *Qur'an*, we are listening to Allah; when we make *du'aa* and *dhikr*, we are talking to Allah; and when we pray, we combine all the above. So when you pray, take your time. Remember beforehand that you are standing before not only the King of Kings, but that you are talking to the One you love more than anyone or anything else.

4. Turn to Him for your needs. When you feel His support, your love for Him will naturally increase.

5. Remember His blessings on you and speak about them. Try listing all the blessings you can think of in your *deen* and in your *dunya* (your world and life).

6. Think of all the difficulties He saved you from.

7. Be around friends who will increase you in Allah's love.

8. Stay away from anything that will distance you from Allah, like sins, bad company, websites with content that decreases your *Imaan* or causes you to sin, and so on.

9. Do the obligatory deeds well, then do the voluntary. Good deeds increase our *Iman* and, in turn, our love of Allah. Be loving and affectionate to others because Allah loves the characteristic of being loving. The Prophet *sallAllahu 'alayhi wa sallam* said, *"The believer is loving and affectionate. There is no good in anyone who is neither loving nor loved by others."* [95]

---

95. Ahmad, Al-Hakim, Al-Bazzar

CHAPTER 7

Al-'Alee, Al-Muta'aal
{The Most High and The Exalted}

ALLAH IS THE MOST HIGH

Allah says,

وَهُوَ ٱلْعَلِيُّ ٱلْعَظِيمُ

"And He is Al-'Alee (The Most High), Al-'Adheem (The Greatest)." [96]

سَبِّحِ ٱسْمَ رَبِّكَ ٱلْأَعْلَى

"Glorify the Name of your Lord, Al-A'laa (the Most High)." [97]

"(He is) the Knower of the unseen and the witnessed, Al-Kabeer (the Grand), Al-Muta'aal (the High / Exalted)." [98]

What does it mean to be *"The Highest"*? With regards to Allah, it includes several meanings:

First, Allah's Being is above all of His creation, which was mentioned in seven different places in the *Qur'an*,

ثُمَّ ٱسْتَوَىٰ عَلَى ٱلْعَرْشِ

"Then He rose above The Throne." [99]

Allah has explained that there are seven heavens, the lowest of them being the skies of our world.

---

96. Surah Al-Baqarah [2:255]
97. Surah Al-A'laa [87:1]
98. Surah Ar-Ra'ad [13:9]
99. Surah Al-A'raaf [7:54], Yunus [10:3], Ar-Ra'ad [13:2], Taha [20:5], Al-Furqaan [25:59], As-Sajdah [32:4], Al-Hadeed [57:4]

The Prophet sallAllahu 'alayhi wa sallam said, "If Allah decrees a command, the angels carrying His throne glorify Him, then the angels in the next nearest heavens glorify Him, and so on until their glorification reaches the angels of the heavens of this world..." [100]

And above the seven heavens is Paradise, the highest level of which is called Al-Firdaws. Allah's throne is above Al-Firdaws, and He is above His throne. So He is the Highest, and nothing is above Him. The Prophet said, "Paradise has a hundred levels, and between each level is like the distance between the heavens and earth. Al-Firdaws is the highest level, and four rivers of Paradise flow from it, and above it is the Throne. So when you ask Allah, ask Him for Al-Firdaws." [101]

There are many other Qur'anic verses and Prophetic sayings that prove that Allah is above the heavens, a few of which are as follows: Allah states,

وَهُوَ ٱلْقَاهِرُ فَوْقَ عِبَادِهِ

"And He is Al-Qahir (the Almighty, the Subduer) above His servants." [102]

He also says,

يَخَافُونَ رَبَّهُم مِّن فَوْقِهِمْ

"They (the angels) fear their Lord, who is above them." [103]

He says,

تَعْرُجُ ٱلْمَلَٰٓئِكَةُ وَٱلرُّوحُ إِلَيْهِ

"The angels and the Spirit (Gabriel) ascend to Him." [104]

This is an essential concept to understand because some people have the misunderstanding or mistaken belief that Allah is everywhere (i.e., physically), even though neither He nor His Prophet sallAllahu 'alayhi wa sallam have ever stated this. Some people go as far as to say that He is within each and every individual. This may even lead to shirk sometimes because some believe that certain righteous people were incarnations of God, or manifestations of God, walking on earth. This is an example of how important it is for us to only confirm what Allah stated about Himself, as we mentioned earlier.

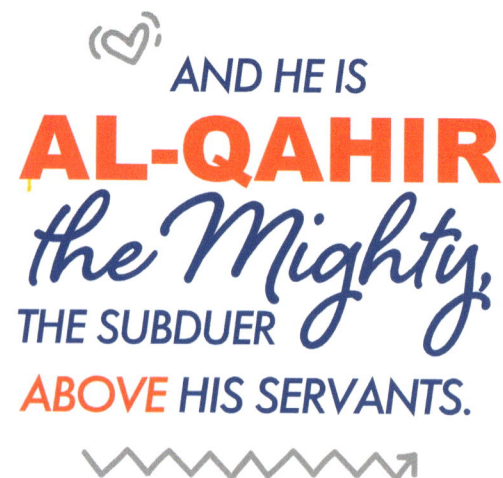
AND HE IS AL-QAHIR the Mighty, THE SUBDUER ABOVE HIS SERVANTS.

---

100. Sahih Muslim
101. Sahih Al-Bukhari
102. Surah Al-An'aam [6:18]
103. Surah An-Nahl [16:50]
104. Surah Al-Ma'aarij [70:4]

HIGHEST LEVEL OF JUSTICE

The second way in which Allah is the Most High and Exalted is with regard to His Names and Attributes. This simply means that Allah's characteristics are greater and loftier than those of anyone else. His characteristics are at the highest level of perfection, completion, and beauty. For example, no matter how fair a human may be, Allah will always be the Most Just and have the highest level of justice. No matter how kind and compassionate a human may be, Allah will always have the highest degree of compassion.

The third way in which Allah is the Most High and Exalted is in His power and authority. His power is above anyone else's in that He alone is able to do absolutely anything. Similarly, His authority and control are above everyone else's authority and control in that nothing can occur without His permission.

Because Allah's Being, Attributes, and authority are above His entire creation, He should then be above everyone and everything else in our hearts and in our lives. The goal of attaining His pleasure is above and beyond that of attaining anyone else's. Since His authority is above everyone else's, His obedience should take precedence over everyone else's. For example, if anyone asks us to do something that will constitute disobedience to Allah, we should obey Him and not that person. Moreover, knowing that Allah is the Most High will cause us to turn to Him for all of our needs, major or minor, since only He can grant them and only He controls everything and everyone. If we fear anything in our future, we should run to Him alone for protection because only He has the power to protect us, and He is more powerful than whatever we fear.

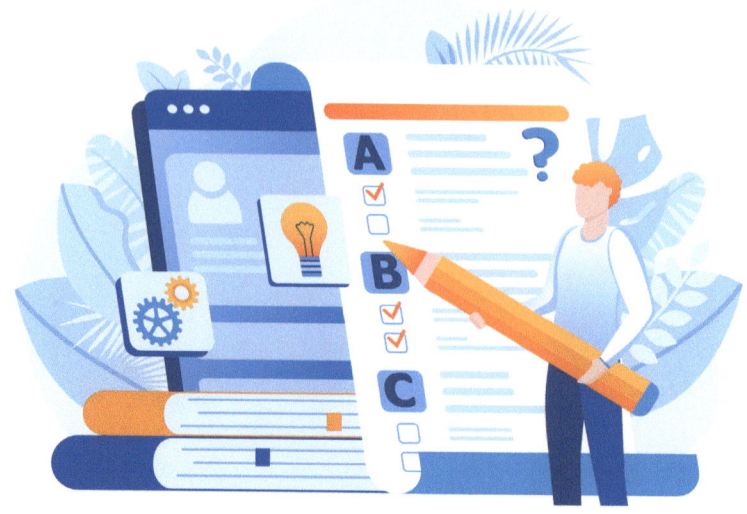

CHAPTER 6&7

REVIEW AND REFLECT QUESTIONS

1

If you were asked who do you love for the sake of Allah? Whose name would come up in your mind? Why do you love for the sake of Allah? How does loving someone for the sake of Allah make the bond between you and them grow?

2

Hamza comes home from his security job at 3:00 am every day. Every time his apartment door opens it makes a big screech that disturbs his neighbors. He contemplates what he should do in order to be respectful of his neighbor and not disturb him. He decides to pay a carpenter to fix the issue with the door. What does this tell you about Hamza's personality?

3

Being truthful is extremely important because it strengthens our relationships, our friendships, and society as a whole. What do you feel is the main cause of why people tend to be dishonest in situations?

4

If your friend tells you, "*Allah is everywhere physically.*" How would you explain where Allah is?

CHAPTER 8

ALLAH IS ONE
Shirk in Allah's Names and Attributes

Shirk, as we have discussed in *Tawheed ur-Ruboobiyyah,* is associating partners with Allah or attributing the qualities of Allah to other things. This is one of the greatest sins, which, depending on the type of shirk and the intention behind it, can take one out of Islam. Many people attribute partners to Allah in His Names and Attributes, and this can take several forms. As we mentioned earlier, although Allah has attributes and His creation may have similar attributes, they are nothing alike. Allah's attributes are limitless and perfect, while people's attributes are limited and imperfect. So Allah can see and hear, and we can see and hear, but there is no comparison between the two. Allah can hear everything all at once, and He can hear sounds that no creature can hear, while we can only hear what is within earshot and within a specific range. Furthermore, as we mentioned, if we added the mercy and compassion of all of the creation that ever existed, it would not equate to even one hundredth of Allah's mercy, and so on.

> قُلْ هُوَ ٱللَّهُ أَحَدٌ
>
> SAY: HE IS ALLAH (THE) ONE.[105]

Surah Al-Ikhlaas

---

105. Surah Al-Ikhlaas [112:1]

1. SHIRK BY LIKENING ALLAH TO HIS CREATION

Oftentimes, people attribute to Allah human traits, which are traits of deficiency or weakness. For example, Christians claim that God is a father who has a son. However, Allah is divine, and He is too exalted and perfect to need or have a child. He is separate and distinct from His creation.

Another example can be found in the Biblical claim that God got tired after creating the heavens and the earth.[106] Tiredness indicates a need for rest, but Allah is free of all need. Allah clearly states,

$$\text{لَا تَأْخُذُهُ سِنَةٌ وَلَا نَوْمٌ}$$

"Neither drowsiness nor sleep overtakes Him." [107]

Furthermore, both the Bible and Torah (which were altered over time) state that God repented for his evil thoughts! [108]

2. SHIRK BY LIKENING THE CREATION TO ALLAH

In this type, people give Allah's creation divine attributes that belong only to Allah, thereby making them equal to Allah in this regard. A few examples of this are as follows:

- **C**hristian belief that Prophet Isa (Jesus), a human, is God.

- **B**elieving that angels, saints, or prophets can answer a person's prayers or protect them from harm is a form of shirk in Allah's Names and Attributes as well.

- **S**ome Shi'ite sects believe that their imams are perfect and infallible, that is, incapable of making any mistakes. [109]

- **B**elieving in good or bad luck charms and omens also includes shirk in Allah's Names and Attributes, in addition to shirk in *Ruboobiyyah*. This is because only Allah is capable of providing us with good (*Ar-Rabb* and *Ar-Razzaq*, the Provider), and only He can repel harm (*Ar-Rabb* and *Al-Hafiz*, the Protector).

- **B**elief in fortune-telling and horoscopes also encompasses shirk in Allah's Names and Attributes. This is because the person attributes to the fortune-teller Allah's attribute of *Knower* of the *unseen*. In other words, only Allah knows the future.

---

106. Genesis [2:2] states: *"And on the seventh day God finished his work which he had done, and he rested on the seventh day from all his work which he had done."* (Holy Bible, Revised Standard Version, Nelson, 1951, p.2; as cited in Philips, B. The Fundamentals of *Tawheed*).
107. Surah Al-Baqarah [2:255]
108. Exodus [32:14]: *"And the Lord repented of the evil which he thought to do to his people."* (as cited in Philips, B. The Fundamentals of *Tawheed*)
109. *"We believe that, like the prophet, an Imam must be infallible, that is to say incapable of making errors or doing wrong, either inwardly or outwardly, from his birth to his death, either intentionally or unintentionally."* (Muhammad Riza Muzaffar, Faith of Shi'a Islam, 1983, as cited in Philips, B. The Fundamentals of *Tawheed*)

CHAPTER 8

REVIEW AND REFLECT QUESTIONS

1

Noor comes to you showing you her new t-shirt. It is very expensive and pretty, but you notice it has the blue eye (an image of an eye used in some cultures to ward off the evil eye and to help protect people, property, etc.) on it. You ask her about it, and she responds that she doesn't believe in the blue eye, so it is ok for her to wear it. What would you say to her?

2

"He who does not know evil will fall into it." How far should we go in learning about the evil of horoscopes? What is sufficient knowledge for a person to know to protect themselves from this form of *shirk*?

3

Your friend is Christian, and he wants to know the difference between how you view God in comparison to how he views God. What key points should you discuss with him that you learned in the beginning of this chapter?

UNIT 2
WORSHIPING ALLAH

UNIT 2

Important Vocabulary

'Abd
Servant

Adhkar
A collection of *du'aas* and Remembrances from the *Sunnah*

Al-'Aleem
The All-Knowing One, The One nothing is absent from His knowledge

Al-Khaaliq
The Creator, The One who brings everything from non-existence to existence.

Al-Ikhlaas
The sincere Intention

An-Niyyah
The intention in one's heart

Ar-Raheem
The Most Merciful

Ar-Rasool
The Messenger (refers to the Prophet Muhammad)

Ayaat
Plural of *Ayah*; verse of the *Qur'an*, also refers to the signs of Allah

Eid-ul-Adha
Festival of Sacrifice in the Islamic month of Dhul-Hijjah

'Ibaadah
The obedience, submission, and devotion to Allah along with the ultimate love for Him

Ilah
God, anything or anyone that is worshipped

Jinn
A creation of Allah made from a smokeless flame of fire

Khawf
Fear

Muslim
The one who practices Islam, the one who submits to Allah

Rajaa'
Hope or Expectation

Rak'ah
A single unit in the prayer (salaah)

Ramadan
The ninth month of the Islamic calendar, the month of fasting

Sadaqah
Defined as true or sincere. Being true to Allah. Refers to to a voluntary deed or an act of kindness done sincerely for Allah.

Salaah
Prayer

Shaytaan
Devil

Sunnah
The way and guidance of the Prophet *sallAllahu 'alayhi wa sallam*

Taghoot
False objects of worship

Tawakkul
To trust and rely on Allah

Tawheed
Allah's Oneness

Tawheed ul-Uloohiyyah
Allah's Oneness in Worship; To attest to the Oneness of Allah and perform all acts of worship solely for Him.

Wahy
Revelation or Inspiration, referring to the *Qur'an* and *Sunnah*

Zakaah
An annual alms that each Muslim is obligated to pay

TABLE OF CONTENTS

UNIT 2 | Worshiping ALLAH

CHAPTER	PG	
09	93	Worshiping Allah Only
10	107	Living Between Hope & Fear
11	113	How Worship is Accepted?

Essential Questions

This unit is designed to help answer the following questions.

1. Why should we worship Allah?
2. How does Allah impact our life?
3. What is the role of revelation over intellect?
4. How can we find a balance between fear and hope?

CHAPTER 9

WORSHIPING ALLAH ONLY
Tawheed ul-Uloohiyyah
[Maintaining Allah's Oneness in His Worship]

WHO KNOWS YOU THE BEST?

Allah is *Al-Khaaliq* (The Creator), The One who brings everything from non-existence to existence. He is also *Al-'Aleem* (The All-Knowing One), The One and Only true god (*Al-Ahad*). Nothing is absent from His knowledge. Is there anyone else who would know you better than your own creator? From Allah's perfect knowledge of how He created us and truly knowing what is best for us, He has given us guidance on how to worship Him. This aspect of *tawheed*, **Tawheed ul-Uloohiyyah** (Allah's Oneness in Worship), can be explained as devoting all acts of worship, both inward and outward, in word and action, to Allah Alone, and not worshiping anything or anyone other than Allah. There are several *ayaat* in the Qur'an where Allah informs us of this. Allah says,

إِنَّنِى أَنَا ٱللَّهُ لَا إِلَٰهَ إِلَّا أَنَا۠ فَٱعْبُدْنِى وَأَقِمِ ٱلصَّلَوٰةَ لِذِكْرِىٓ

"Indeed, I am Allah. There is no one worthy of worship except Me, so worship Me and establish prayer for My remembrance." [1]

وَلَقَدْ بَعَثْنَا فِى كُلِّ أُمَّةٍ رَّسُولًا أَنِ ٱعْبُدُوا۟ ٱللَّهَ وَٱجْتَنِبُوا۟ ٱلطَّٰغُوتَ

"And We certainly sent into every nation a messenger, [saying], "Worship Allah and avoid taghoot (false objects of worship)." [2]

---
1. Surah Taha [20:14]
2. Surah An-Nahl [16:36]

The Importance of Tawheed ul-Uloohiyyah

Tawheed ul-Uloohiyyah was the main call to Allah of the Prophet *sallAllahu 'alayhi wa salaam*. The people of *Quraysh* all recognized Allah's Lordship, but they worshipped and devoted their actions to others besides Allah. It is not befitting to believe in Allah's Lordship, His Names and Attributes, and then direct one's worship partially or fully to someone else. This branch of *tawheed* is very important to grasp because acceptance of all of our acts of worship is based upon this understanding, and our success in the Hereafter is dependent upon it. If we don't do our acts solely for Him, none of them will be accepted. Allah says in the *Qur'an*,

وَقَدِمْنَآ إِلَىٰ مَا عَمِلُوا مِنْ عَمَلٍ فَجَعَلْنَٰهُ هَبَآءً مَّنثُورًا

"And We will approach [i.e., regard] what they have done of deeds and make them as dust dispersed." 3

The above verse is drawing attention to those who will come on the Day of Judgment thinking they have so many good deeds, but they will find that all their good deeds are made into dust and worthless because they may have directed parts of their worship to someone other than Allah or their actions were not in accordance with what the Prophet *sallAllahu 'alayhi wa sallam* brought. In order to be successful in this world and the Hereafter, we have to wholeheartedly accept Allah as the Only One to be worshipped, all acts of worship must be directed to Him Alone, and we must always give precedence to following the *Sunnah* in our daily lives.

ACKNOWLEDGMENT WITHOUT SUBMISSION

Most people acknowledge Allah is great. However, the challenge truly is to put that acknowledgment into action by submitting completely to Allah. If we acknowledge a human being is smart and successful, it is natural to respect and want to follow that individual. When we acknowledge Allah is The Greatest and The All-Knowing, it should create in us an awe, reverence, and respect for Him. And that should cause us to totally submit to His commandments and prohibitions.

KEY POINT: As Muslims, we don't just acknowledge, but we must submit as well.

---

3. Surah Al-Furqaan [25:23]

> وَمَآ أَرْسَلْنَا مِن قَبْلِكَ مِن رَّسُولٍ إِلَّا نُوحِىٓ إِلَيْهِ أَنَّهُۥ لَآ إِلَٰهَ إِلَّآ أَنَا۠ فَٱعْبُدُونِ
>
> WE NEVER SENT A MESSENGER BEFORE YOU WITHOUT REVEALING TO HIM: THERE IS NO GOD EXCEPT ME, SO WORSHIP ME." [4]

Surah Al-Anbiyaa'

What is 'Ibaadah?

'Ibaadah is commonly defined as the worship of Allah. On a wider scope, it refers to everything that Allah asks us to do while performing it with complete **love, obedience,** and **submission** to Him. Ibn *Taymiyyah* [5] *rahimahullaah* explained it beautifully when he said, "**Ibaadah** *is a collective term for everything that Allah loves and is pleased with from amongst sayings and inward and outward actions."* [6] In other words, *ibaadah* is not limited to just rituals in Islam, but rather it is inclusive of all acts of the heart, body, and tongue that are done solely for the pleasure of Allah.

---

4. Surah Al-Anbiyaa' [21:25]
5. Famous Scholar of *hadith*, tafseer, and jurisprudence (d.1328 C.E)
6. Majmu' Al-Fataawa

THIS IS ALSO 'IBAADAH...

'IBAADAH OF THE HEART

- To have good thoughts about Allah.
- To have good assumptions of the people around us.
- To keep our heart clean from the diseases of the heart like jealousy, envy, holding gudges, etc.

'IBAADAH OF THE BODY

- To use our legs and hands in acts that will please Allah.
- To help someone without expecting any favors or rewards in return.
- To not use our hands or legs to physically harm a creation of Allah.

'IBAADAH OF THE TONGUE

- To keep the tongue engaged in good acts for the sake of Allah.
- To use the tongue to recite the *Qur'an* and make *du'aa*.
- To speak good about others and to refrain from backbiting, mocking, or using abusive language.

YOU ARE DOING 'IBAADAH

1. **YOU THINK** good of others for the pleasure of Allah, and you are happy at the success of others.

2. **YOU SPEAK** in a good manner, refraining from using abusive language.

3. **YOU ATTEND** the *masjid* purely for Allah's pleasure and coming closer to Him.

4. **YOU HELP** someone so that Allah will be pleased with you and not because that person will return the favor to you one day.

5. **YOU EARN** a livelihood in accordance with regulations of the *Shari'ah*.

6. **YOU TAKE CARE** of your guests when they visit and serve them generously, seeking reward from Allah.

7. **YOU GUIDE** people to do what is good and keep away from unlawful things.

8. **YOU REMOVE** a harmful object from the ground to protect others from getting hurt.

How Do I Show My Love to Allah?

We show our love to Allah by **obeying or submitting to** His commandments from the *Qur'an* and following the *Sunnah* of the Prophet *sallAllahu 'alayhi wa sallam*. As Muslims, we understand that *Sunnah* is also a revelation from Allah in the words of the Prophet *sallAllahu 'alayhi wa sallam*. Allah says in the *Qur'an*,

قُلْ إِن كُنتُمْ تُحِبُّونَ ٱللَّهَ فَٱتَّبِعُونِى يُحْبِبْكُمُ ٱللَّهُ وَيَغْفِرْ لَكُمْ ذُنُوبَكُمْ وَٱللَّهُ غَفُورٌ رَّحِيمٌ

"Say, [O Muhammad], "If you should love Allah, then follow me, [so] Allah will love you and forgive you your sins. And Allah is Forgiving and Merciful." [7]

We also show our love by **abstaining** from that which Allah has forbidden us from doing. Allah says in the *Qur'an*,

وَمَآ ءَاتَىٰكُمُ ٱلرَّسُولُ فَخُذُوهُ وَمَا نَهَىٰكُمْ عَنْهُ فَٱنتَهُوا۟

" ...And whatever the Messenger has given you - take; and what he has forbidden you - refrain from..." [8]

---

7. Ale-'Imraan [3:31]
8. Surah Al-Hashr [59:7]

Journey to Allah Series **Who Is Allah?** | 97

AN EMOTIONAL DETOX

Finding Inner Peace

Worshiping Allah with love is an amazing emotional detox. Why so? There are many people who are confused and clueless about what to do. They aimlessly wander in their lives trying to find guidance, getting stressed out and depressed about which fads to follow, where to socialize, and how to find inner peace, not realizing that the One who has created them has provided them with a clear roadmap for life.

On the other hand, a Muslim realizes that Allah loves him or her tremendously and that whatever Allah has asked the Muslim to do is the best for him or her. A Muslim, thus, spends his or her energy in worshiping Him with confidence, peace, and happiness.

The love of and belief in Allah takes the guesswork out of life and emotionally detoxes a person! This makes the person peaceful and content.

What Does Submitting to Allah Mean?

Submission to Allah means **submitting with your heart, your tongue, and your body** to that which Allah has asked you to do and to stay away from what Allah has asked us to stay away from. Since Allah is *Al-Khaaliq* (The Creator) and He is *Al-'Aleem* (The All-Knowing), he knows what is best for us, and it only makes sense for us to submit to Him completely without any questioning. After all, that is the definition of a Muslim - the one who consciously submits to Allah with sincerity.

Allah mentions to us in the *Qur'an*,

قُلْ إِنَّ صَلَاتِى وَنُسُكِى وَمَحْيَاىَ وَمَمَاتِى لِلَّهِ رَبِّ ٱلْعَٰلَمِينَ لَا شَرِيكَ لَهُ وَبِذَٰلِكَ أُمِرْتُ وَأَنَا۠ أَوَّلُ ٱلْمُسْلِمِينَ

"Say, 'Indeed, my prayer, my rites of sacrifice, my living and my dying are for Allah, Lord of the worlds. No partner has He. And this I have been commanded, and I am the first [among you] of the Muslims (i.e., those who submit)...'" [9]

---
9. Surah Al-An'aam [6:162-163]

I CAN SUBMIT BY...

1 PRAYING MY FIVE *SALAAHS*,

not as a simple chore, but with an understanding that it is good for me to pray those *salaahs* on time.

2 LISTENING TO MY PARENTS,

even when I don't really feel like it, because Allah has told me to do so and it is good for me.

3 FASTING IN THE MONTH OF RAMADAN,

not with the intention to lose weight or to become physically fit, but only because Allah has commanded me to fast and it is good for me to do so.

4 BEING KIND TO SOMEONE WHO IS BEING MEAN TO ME,

not because I am weak, but because Allah guided me to do so, and that is good for me.

LET'S EXPLORE HOW **GREAT PEOPLE** BEFORE US SUBMITTED TO ALLAH

THE SUBMISSION OF IBRAHIM 'ALAYHIS SALAAM

Ibrahim *'alayhis salaam* was asked to slaughter his very own son. He did not let his intellect ask *"why"* or *"what!?"* He and his son (Isma'il *'alayhimus salaam*) submitted to Allah. Allah says in the *Qur'an*,

فَلَمَّا بَلَغَ مَعَهُ ٱلسَّعْىَ قَالَ يَٰبُنَىَّ إِنِّىٓ أَرَىٰ فِى ٱلْمَنَامِ أَنِّىٓ أَذْبَحُكَ فَٱنظُرْ مَاذَا تَرَىٰ قَالَ يَٰٓأَبَتِ ٱفْعَلْ مَا تُؤْمَرُ سَتَجِدُنِىٓ إِن شَآءَ ٱللَّهُ مِنَ ٱلصَّٰبِرِينَ

فَلَمَّآ أَسْلَمَا وَتَلَّهُۥ لِلْجَبِينِ

وَنَٰدَيْنَٰهُ أَن يَٰٓإِبْرَٰهِيمُ

قَدْ صَدَّقْتَ ٱلرُّءْيَآ إِنَّا كَذَٰلِكَ نَجْزِى ٱلْمُحْسِنِينَ

"And when he reached with him [the age of] exertion, he said, "O my son, indeed, I have seen in a dream that I [must] sacrifice you, so see what you think." **He said, "O my father, do as you are commanded. You will find me, if Allah wills, of the steadfast."** *And when they had both submitted and he put him down upon his forehead, We called to him, "O Abraham, You have fulfilled the vision." Indeed, We thus reward the doers of good."* [10]

Today, thousands of years later, billions of Muslims all over the world commemorate their act of submission to Allah on *Eid-ul-Adha*.

THE SUBMISSION OF MUSA 'ALAYHIS SALAAM

Musa *'alayhis salaam* and his followers were being chased by the Pharaoh. When He was commanded by Allah to strike the sea with his staff. Allah says in the *Qur'an*,

فَأَوْحَيْنَآ إِلَىٰ مُوسَىٰٓ أَنِ ٱضْرِب بِّعَصَاكَ ٱلْبَحْرَ فَٱنفَلَقَ فَكَانَ كُلُّ فِرْقٍ كَٱلطَّوْدِ ٱلْعَظِيمِ

"Then We inspired to Musa, **"Strike with your staff the sea**,*" and it parted, and each portion was like a great towering mountain."* [11]

He did not question or argue. He did what Allah asked him to do. The sea split. Musa *'alayhis salaam* submitted to Allah, and his people crossed the sea and were saved from Pharaoh and his people.

---

10. Surah As-Saaffaat [37:102-105]
11. Surah Ash-Shu'araa' [26:63]

THE SUBMISSION OF ABU BAKR *RADHIALLAHU 'ANHU*

Abu Bakr *radhiAllahu 'anhu* used to financially support his relative, Mistah *radhiAllahu 'anhu*. During the famous incident where Abu Bakr's daughter, Aisha *radhiAllahu 'anha* was accused of committing something she never did, Mistah was one of the people who spread rumors about it. Abu Bakr *radhiAllahu 'anhu* was deeply hurt and wanted to stop his financial support for Mistah *radhiAllahu 'anhu*. But Allah commanded him to pardon and overlook. Allah says in the *Qur'an*,

وَلَا يَأْتَلِ أُولُوا ٱلْفَضْلِ مِنكُمْ وَٱلسَّعَةِ أَن يُؤْتُوٓا۟ أُو۟لِى ٱلْقُرْبَىٰ وَٱلْمَسَٰكِينَ وَٱلْمُهَٰجِرِينَ فِى سَبِيلِ ٱللَّهِ وَلْيَعْفُوا۟ وَلْيَصْفَحُوٓا۟ أَلَا تُحِبُّونَ أَن يَغْفِرَ ٱللَّهُ لَكُمْ وَٱللَّهُ غَفُورٌ رَّحِيمٌ

*"And let not those of virtue among you and wealth swear not to give [aid] to their relatives and the needy and the emigrants for the cause of Allah, **and let them pardon and overlook.** Would you not like that Allah should forgive you? And Allah is Forgiving and Merciful."* [12]

Abu Bakr's immediate response, without any hesitation or argumentation, was to forgive him. He immediately resumed his financial support for Mistah. To this date, we recite these ayaat from the *Qur'an* while remembering Abu Bakr *radhiAllahu 'anhu* and his act of submission.

IBLIS DID NOT SUBMIT

When Allah created Adam *'alayhis salaam* and asked everyone to prostrate to Adam *'alayhis salaam*, all the angels complied. But Iblis [13] tried to use his intellect to undermine. The response of Iblis was mentioned in the *Qur'an*,

قَالَ أَنَا۠ خَيْرٌ مِّنْهُ خَلَقْتَنِى مِن نَّارٍ وَخَلَقْتَهُۥ مِن طِينٍ

"[Satan] said, "I am better than him. You created me from fire and created him from clay" [i.e., earth]..." [14]

Iblis, with his limited intellect, disobeyed Allah because he felt his creation was better than the angels. His prideful disobedience to Allah was the cause for him to be expelled from the heavens and cursed.

---

12. Surah An-Nur [24:22]
13. Iblis, commonly known as *Shaytaan*, as mentioned in the *Qur'an*, was a jinn who was among the angels when Allah ordered everyone to prostrate to Adam *'alayhis salaam*.
14. Surah Al-A'raaf [7:12]

WHY SHOULD WE SUBMIT?

Allah's knowledge is infinite. Ours is not. We end up hurting ourselves physically, emotionally, and spiritually when we don't listen to Him. Just like when a parent tells a child not to place his hand on an open fire. Nevertheless, the child uses his intellect to touch it because it seems attractive with its bright yellow, blue, and orange flames. Similarly, when we decide to use our intellect over what Allah has asked us to do, we don't hurt Allah; we only end up hurting ourselves. We want a good and easy life, and to get that, we should submit wholeheartedly to that which Allah has commanded us to do.

Allah says,

مَنْ عَمِلَ صَالِحًا مِّن ذَكَرٍ أَوْ أُنثَىٰ وَهُوَ مُؤْمِنٌ فَلَنُحْيِيَنَّهُ حَيَاةً طَيِّبَةً وَلَنَجْزِيَنَّهُمْ أَجْرَهُم بِأَحْسَنِ مَا كَانُوا يَعْمَلُونَ

"Whoever does righteousness, whether male or female, while he is a believer - We will surely cause him to live a good life, and We will surely give them their reward [in the Hereafter] according to the best of what they used to do." [15]

---
15. Surah An-Nahl [16:97]

WHAT IS THE PROPER USE OF OUR INTELLECT?

Allah has given us our intellect as a blessing. We use our intellect to make sense out of what goes on around us and to understand what Allah has asked us to do and how to carry it out. However, what if something that Allah has asked us to do doesn't make sense to us? Now what? Who wins? Our intellect, or what Allah has asked?

'Ali radhiAllahu 'anhu said, "If the religion were based upon one's opinion, one might expect the bottom of the leather sock to be wiped instead of the top. I have seen the Messenger of Allah, peace and blessings be upon him, wiping over the upper part of his leather socks." [16]

The statement above is a perfect example of comprehending that our religion isn't always based on our human intellect or what makes sense, but it is based on what Allah has guided us to do. Our mind is limited, and thus we cannot comprehend the wisdom behind every guideline of Allah. But we do know that out of Allah's love and mercy, He would only ask us to do what is best for us.

---

16. Abu Dawood

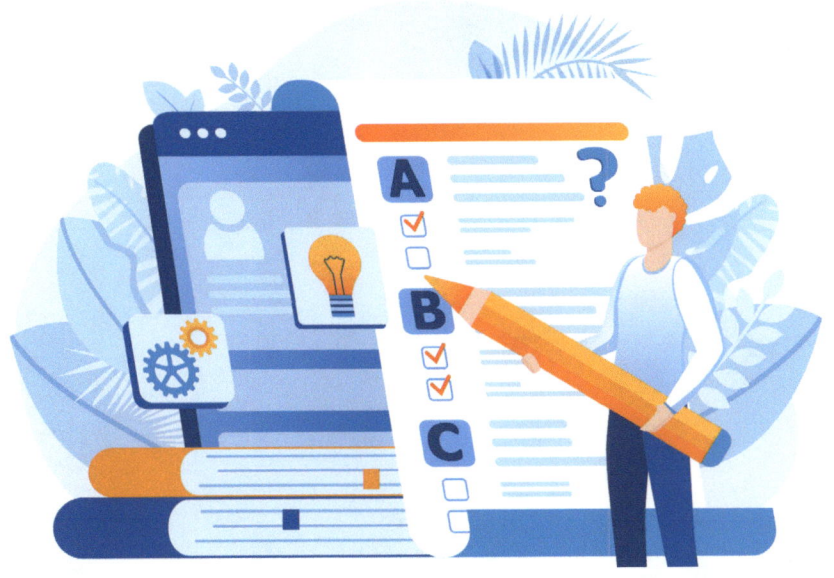

CHAPTER 9
REVIEW AND REFLECT QUESTIONS

1

Fasting is obligatory on a person once they attain puberty. Some parents believe if their child is not emotionally or spiritually ready to fast, then they shouldn't have to. What would you advise a parent who is taking the obligation of fasting into their own hands?

2

Sarah finishes her *salaah* with a sigh of relief and the statement, *"I am done! Finally! Now I can relax."* What might that comment reflect about Sarah and her relationship with her *salaah*?

3

Allah has created us, and out of His mercy, He has given us a complete guide on what to do and what not to do. It is easy to acknowledge Allah's greatness, yet the challenge is in submitting to Him completely. How does submitting to Allah benefit us in our daily lives?

CHAPTER 10

LIVING BETWEEN HOPE & FEAR

(AR-RAJAA' & AL-KHAWF)

Islam teaches us to worship Allah not only out of love for Him but with a healthy balance of both hope and fear. Understanding how to combine these two qualities into our *ibaadah* will help us in improving our worship. Allah says in the Qur'an,

إِنَّهُمْ كَانُوا يُسَارِعُونَ فِي الْخَيْرَاتِ وَيَدْعُونَنَا رَغَبًا وَرَهَبًا وَكَانُوا لَنَا خَاشِعِينَ

*"... Indeed, they used to hasten to good deeds and **supplicate Us in hope and fear**, and they were to Us humbly submissive."* [17]

Rajaa' means hope, and specifically when it comes to our *'ibaadah*, it is referring to the hope a believer has in Allah accepting their good deeds and their repentance. Hope in Allah helps motivate us to do good deeds, seeking His love and reward in this world and the hereafter. **Khawf** means fear, and it is the fear the believer has that Allah might not accept from them their *ibaadah*, good deeds, or forgive them. Fear of Allah leads us to strive to do better. It helps us to think twice before committing a sin and helps us stay away from acting upon something that will lead us towards the hellfire.

---

17. Surah Al-Anbiyaa' [21:90]

We also have to balance between the extremes of hope and fear. Too much hope can make us neglectful towards Allah's commands, and too much fear can make us despair in His mercy. Ibn Al-Qayyim [18] rahimahullaah beautifully described how the balance of hope and fear should be in the hearts of the believers.

He said, *"The heart on its journey towards Allah the Exalted is like that of a bird.* **Love** *is its head, and* **fear** *and* **hope** *are its two wings. When the head is healthy, then the two wings will fly well. When the head is cut off, the bird will die. When either of two wings is damaged, the bird becomes vulnerable to every hunter and predator."* [19]

Having Hope in Allah

As Muslims, we should always try our best to do our deeds for Allah and seek his pleasure. And by doing so, we should have hope that if we did it with sincerity and did our best, Allah would accept it from us. Similarly, if we repent to Allah with sincerity, we should also have hope that Allah will forgive us. A believer should never lose hope in *Ar-Raheem* (The Most Merciful) and always be in a state where he is thinking positively of his creator. The Prophet *sallAllahu 'alayhi wa sallam* said:

"Allah (the Most Merciful) said, **'I am as My servant thinks (expects) I am**. *I am with him when he remembers Me. If he remembers Me personally, I remember him personally; if he remembers Me in an assembly, I mention him in an assembly greater than that. If he draws near to Me a hand's length, I draw near to him an arm's length. And if he comes to Me walking, I come to him hastily.'"* [20]

قُلْ يَٰعِبَادِىَ ٱلَّذِينَ أَسْرَفُوا۟ عَلَىٰٓ أَنفُسِهِمْ لَا تَقْنَطُوا۟ مِن رَّحْمَةِ ٱللَّهِ

SAY: "O MY SERVANTS WHO HAVE TRANSGRESSED GREATLY AGAINST THEIR OWN SOULS! DO NOT DESPAIR OF THE MERCY OF ALLAH" [21]

Surah Az-Zumar

---

18. Famous scholar of *fiqh*, *'aqeedah* and *hadith*
19. Madarij As-Salikeen (A book written by the famous 13th century scholar Ibn Al-Qayyim Al-Jawziyyah)
20. Sahih Al-Bukhari
21. Surah Az-Zumar [39:53]

Having Fear of Allah

Having fear of Allah is to fear disobeying, displeasing, or disappointing your Creator and falling into sins that may lead to His wrath or punishment. This type of fear can be compared to a fear of someone you love dearly (like your parents, relatives, friends, etc.). Someone you do not want to upset because making them upset would ruin your relationship with them. Similarly, fearing Allah is something positive, as it leads you towards coming closer to Allah by abstaining from what He has asked us not to do. Ibn Taymiyyah *rahimahullaah* said, *"The commendable khawf (fear) is what restrains you from the prohibitions of Allah."* [22]

Fearing Allah can be increased when we learn more about Allah and what Allah requires from us. Ibn Masud *radhiAllahu 'anhu* said: *"Fear of Allah is sufficient indication of knowledge. Lack of fear of Allah is due to a person's lack of knowledge of Him. The most knowledgeable of people are those who fear Allah the most. If a person knows Allah, he will feel more shy before Him, will fear Him more, and love Him more. The more his knowledge increases, the more his shyness, fear, and love of Him increases."* [23]

Beware of *Shaytaan's* Trap!

If you are worshiping Allah, *shaytaan* is hard at work to stop you from doing so. Allah mentions to us the promise of *shaytaan*

تَتَجَافَىٰ جُنُوبُهُمْ عَنِ ٱلْمَضَاجِعِ يَدْعُونَ رَبَّهُمْ خَوْفًا وَطَمَعًا وَمِمَّا رَزَقْنَٰهُمْ يُنفِقُونَ

THEY ARISE FROM THEIR BEDS AND THEY SUPPLICATE THEIR LORD IN FEAR AND HOPE AND THEY SPEND FROM WHAT WE HAVE PROVIDED THEM. [24]

Surah As-Sajdah

misguiding the believers in the *Qur'an*,

قَالَ فَبِمَآ أَغْوَيْتَنِى لَأَقْعُدَنَّ لَهُمْ صِرَٰطَكَ ٱلْمُسْتَقِيمَ ثُمَّ لَءَاتِيَنَّهُم مِّنۢ بَيْنِ أَيْدِيهِمْ وَمِنْ خَلْفِهِمْ وَعَنْ أَيْمَٰنِهِمْ وَعَن شَمَآئِلِهِمْ ۖ وَلَا تَجِدُ أَكْثَرَهُمْ شَٰكِرِينَ

"[Satan] said, "Because You have put me in error, I will surely sit in wait for them [i.e., mankind] on Your straight path. Then I will come to them from before them and from behind them and on their right and on their left, and You will not find most of them grateful [to You]."" [25]

As you improve yourself in finding the right balance of hope and fear, *shaytaan* will work hard to take you to an extreme of being fearful and hopeful.

---

22. Famous Scholar of *hadith*, *tafseer*, and jurisprudence (d.1328)
23. Tareeq Al-Hijratayn
24. Surah As-Sajdah [32:16]
25. Surah Al-A'raaf [7:16-17]

ACTIVITY

Look at the scenarios in the left column below. In the right column, write H (for hopeful) and F (for fearful) to describe whether or not the person is going to an extreme in being hopeful or fearful.

SCENARIOS

Extreme
H (hopeful or F (fearful)

AHMAD THINKS: Goodness is only in my heart. As long as I feel good about *salaah*, I don't have to pray. Allah is merciful and knows my heart. He will reward me for my feelings. No need to pray!

FATIMA THINKS: I always mess up. I try, but I always do bad. I am no good. There is no point in trying to do good things. I give up. Allah will not accept it anyway.

MUKHTAR ARGUES: I live in the west. I have to go with the flow and do what everyone does. I am going to have a girlfriend. Allah is merciful; He knows I am only checking her out so I can decide whether or not to marry her. He is not going to punish me. After all, everyone is doing it.

KHADIJA SUGGESTS: Hijab is just a symbol. The real hijab is in the heart. If I don't wear the hijab in the west, it is because I don't want to look odd, Allah will understand. He is very Kind. He is very Forgiving. As long as He knows that I mean well, He will not punish me.

ZAHRA THINKS: I have done so many bad deeds. I can't stop myself from doing them. Cheating, stealing, lying, hurting people - you name it, I have done it all. There is no way Allah will even look at me. There is no use in me trying to become better. It is not going to happen. I am going to be punished anyway.

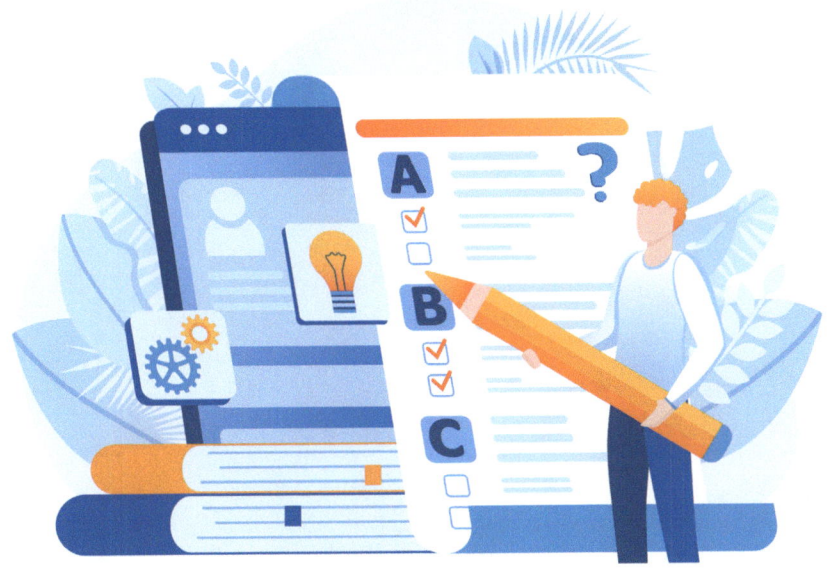

CHAPTER 10
REVIEW AND REFLECT QUESTIONS

1

Akram was playing basketball at the back of the *masjid*. He hears the *adhaan* but is feeling lazy to pray. He tells his friend that Allah is forgiving and that he'll pray at home. His friend has ten minutes till the *salaah* starts; what important point should he share with Akram about missing his *salaah*? How is *Tawheed ul-Uloohiyyah* applied here by Akram?

2

What are two examples of something Allah has asked us to do or stay away from, but many today find difficult to do? How does knowing *Tawheed Al-Uloohiyyah* help change that?

3

Our thoughts have a powerful way to determine our feelings and ultimately affect how we behave. We know that a Muslim must have a balance of both hope and fear in Allah in order for them to live in this world. What steps can you take to find that balance?

CHAPTER 11

HOW WORSHIP IS ACCEPTED?

The scholars of Islam have mentioned that for acts to be accepted and rewarded by Allah, they have to meet two main conditions;

1. **SINCERITY** (*Ikhlaas*)
2. **SUNNAH** (following the way of the Prophet *sallAllahu 'alayhi wa sallam*).

Abu 'Ali Al-Fudayl [26] *rahimahullah* explains how actions will be accepted when someone asked him what was the meaning of *'best in deeds?'* He replied:

'To make it sincere and correct.' He was asked: *'What is meant by making it sincere and correct?'* He replied: *'If a deed is done sincerely but not correctly, it will not be accepted. And if it is done correctly but not sincerely, it will not be accepted—until it is done both sincerely and correctly.'* It was said: *'O Abu 'Ali, what is sincerity and what is correct?'* He replied: **'Sincerity is that the deeds are done purely for Allah, and correct is that it is done according to the Sunnah.'** [27]

---

26. Famous scholar of *hadith* (d. 803 C.E)
27. 'Ilam Al-Muwwaqin (An encyclopedia prepared by Ibn Al-Qayyim Al-Jawziyyah, in which he discusses jurisprudence, its principles and history.)

CONDITION 1
SINCERITY (AL-IKHLAAS)

Ikhlaas can be defined as sincerity or purity. The first condition for our worship to be accepted by Allah is that it is done purely for His sake with sincerity and seeking alone His reward and pleasure. Allah mentions about this sincerity in the following verse,

وَمَآ أُمِرُوٓا۟ إِلَّا لِيَعْبُدُوا۟ ٱللَّهَ مُخْلِصِينَ لَهُ ٱلدِّينَ حُنَفَآءَ وَيُقِيمُوا۟ ٱلصَّلَوٰةَ وَيُؤْتُوا۟ ٱلزَّكَوٰةَ وَذَٰلِكَ دِينُ ٱلْقَيِّمَةِ

"And they were not commanded except to worship Allah, [being] sincere to Him in religion, inclining to truth, and to establish prayer and to give zakah. And that is the correct religion." [28]

Check Your *Niyyah* (Intention)!

No matter how good of an action we do, it will not be accepted if it is done for someone other than Allah. That is why we must keep purifying our intentions before performing good deeds. Our intention should only be to please Allah and seek His pleasure and reward. We must fight any mixed intentions we have where we are doing an act for Allah but also trying to impress someone else or for personal gain.

---

28. Surah Al-Bayyinah [98:5]

ACTIVITY

Identify the mistake(s) in the following scenarios:

1

Walid donates $50,000 at a fundraiser and then announces to everyone on social media that he has donated this amount of money. What should Walid have asked himself before announcing the amount of his donation?

2

Bayan gets involved in humanitarian work and constantly tells people about all the people she has helped. She enjoys her social media following and the likes she gets and and constantly tells people about all the good she does. What should Bayan have asked herself before sharing all her humanitarian efforts?

3

Ahmad recites the *Qur'an* beautifully. Whenever he recites the *Qur'an*, he records himself, puts it up on the internet, and waits for people to give him positive feedback about his recitation. What should Ahmad have asked himself before posting his recitation on the Internet?

> **DID YOU KNOW?**
>
> You get rewarded just by your intention, even if you didn't fulfill it! The Prophet *sallAllahu 'alayhi wa sallam* said, "Whosoever intends to do a good deed but does not do it, Allah records it with Himself as a complete good deed; but if he intends it and does it, Allah records it with Himself as ten good deeds, up to seven hundred times, or more than that. But if he intends to do an evil deed; and does not do it, Allah records it as a complete good deed; but if he intends it and does it, Allah records it down as only one single evil deed? [29] Allah is truly loving and merciful to us!

CONDITION 2
FOLLOWING THE SUNNAH

The second condition for any act of worship to be accepted by Allah is that it must be in accordance with the **Sunnah** of the Prophet *sallAllahu 'alayhi wa sallam*. It was narrated that the Prophet *sallAllahu 'alayhi wa sallam* said,

"Whoever does any action that is not in accordance with this matte of ours (i.e., Islam), will have it rejected." [30]

Ibn Rajab *rahimahullaah* [31] said: *"This hadith forms one of the most important principles of Islam. It is like a scale for weighing up deeds according to their outward appearance, just as the hadith says, 'The reward of deeds depends upon the intentions'* [32] *is the means of weighing up the inner nature of deeds. Just as every action that is not intended for the sake of Allah brings no reward to the one who does it, so too every deed which is not in accordance with the command of Allah and His Messenger will also be rejected and thrown back at the one who does it. Everyone who innovates in Islam something for which Allah and His Messenger have not granted permission, that thing has nothing to do with Islam."* [33]

In another *hadith* the Prophet *sallAllahu 'alayhi wa sallam* told us,

"There is nothing that would bring you closer to Jannah except that I have commanded you to do. And there is nothing that would remove you farther from hell fire except that I have forbidden you from it." [34]

---

29. Sahih Al-Bukhari and Sahih Muslim
30. Sahih Muslim
31. Famous Muslim Scholar (d.1393 C.E)
32. Sahih Al-Bukhari and Sahih Muslim
33. *Jami'Al-'Uloom wal-Hikam* (Ibn Rajab's famous commentary on fifty *hadith*. Every *hadith* is one of those considered by scholars essential to know.)
34. Al-Hakim, Al-Bayhaqi

Therefore, no matter what we do, how many actions we do or even how sincerely we do them, it will not be accepted unless those actions are in accordance with what the Prophet *sallAllahu 'alayhi wa sallam* brought.

 **ACTIVITY** — Identify which of the following acts are from the *Sunnah* and which are not from the *Sunnah*.

YES | NO

1. **RECITING** Ayat-ul-Kursi 786x
2. **PRAYING** two *rak'ahs* before *fajr*
3. **TURNING** off the lights to make *du'aa*
4. **RECITING** Qur'an for the dead
5. **CELEBRATING** the Prophet's Birthday
6. **MAKING** good intentions
7. **REMEMBERING** Allah after *salaah*
8. **PERFORMING** ten *'umrahs*
9. **MAKING** *hajj* for a deceased Muslim
10. **WEARING** a talisman for protection

DID YOU KNOW?

That both the Qur'an and the Sunnah fall under wahy (revelation or inspiration); the Sunnah is all that has been related from the Messenger sallAllahu 'alayhi wa sallam from his statements, actions, tacit approvals, personality, physical description, and life.

Allah says in the Qur'an,

وَمَآ ءَاتَىٰكُمُ ٱلرَّسُولُ فَخُذُوهُ وَمَا نَهَىٰكُمْ عَنْهُ فَٱنتَهُوا۟

"And whatever the Messenger has given you - take; and what he has forbidden you - refrain from..." [35]

When Your Desires Become Your God

If someone were to ask you, *"Do you worship other Ilahs (Gods)?"* You will most likely respond with a resounding, *"No!"* That is because you know very well that you only bow or prostrate to Allah. Worship is more than just the physical and ritual actions we engage in, like prayer, fasting, etc. If you prioritize something over Allah, if you love something or someone more than Allah, or if you prefer something over Allah's commandments, then in essence, you are worshiping that thing or being.

Allah and His Messenger, sallAllahu 'alayhi wa sallam, warn us of some of these 'gods' that people may take. As you look through the following examples, think about your own relationship with Allah and reflect on whether you sometimes fall into any of these categories.

---

35. Surah Al-Hashr [59:7]

EXAMPLES

"Have you seen he who has taken as his god his [own] desire, and Allah has sent him astray due to knowledge and has set a seal upon his hearing and his heart and put over his vision a veil? So who will guide him after Allah? Then will you not be reminded?" [36]

'Adi ibn Hatim *radhiAllahu 'anhu* reported: I came to the Prophet *sallAllahu 'alayhi wa sallam*, while I had a crucifix of gold around my neck. The Prophet said, *"O 'Adi! Remove this idol from yourself!"* I heard him reciting the verse in Surah At-Tawbah, *"They have taken their priests and rabbis as Lords besides Allah."* [37] The Prophet said, *"As for them, they did not worship them, but rather when they made something lawful for them, they considered it lawful. When they made something unlawful for them, they considered it unlawful."* [38]

"And [yet], among the people are those who take other than Allah as equals [to Him]. They love them as they [should] love Allah. But those who believe are stronger in love for Allah." [39]

---

36. Surah Al-Jaathiyah [45:23]
37. At-Tawbah [9:31]
38. At-Tirmidhi
39. Al-Baqarah [2:165]

EVERYDAY SCENARIOS

▶ You sometimes get annoyed at the things your parents say or ask you to do. At times you get so frustrated that you respond back to them in an angry way. You have learned to be kind to your parents, but you **feel** so frustrated at times that you want to just respond to them. What key point should a person consider in regards to being unkind to their parents?

▶ You see civil rights movements advocating for an "alternative way of life," which they want everyone to accept. You hear people sympathizing and supporting them in what they are doing, and promoting their way of life. You have a choice to make: Would you prefer a man-made, ever-changing movement over the divine, stable law of Allah?

▶ You love sports. You can watch it all day long. You consider athletes as cool people with fashionable hairstyles, clothes, and a charming personality. You want to be like them. You get really sad when something bad happens to them. When you are watching them play, you miss your salaah or ignore what your parents may be telling you, or the *Qur'an* assignment that you had to complete. Is this type of love what Allah wants from us?

WHAT'S ONLY FOR ALLAH

There are 5 types of worship that are dedicated to Allah alone.

1. BELIEF

No one other than Allah has the right to be worshipped.

2. ACTIONS OF THE HEART

Certain actions of the heart should only be dedicated to Allah. These include:

TRUST ▸ We can only truly depend and rely on Allah. Other people or things may be used as means to achieve our goals, however, at the end, we must believe in our hearts that we can only accomplish what we strive for with the help of Allah.

FEAR ▸ We may have a natural fear of things that are dangerous (heights, wild animals, etc.), but ultimately, we should only fear Allah and His punishment.

LOVE ▸ We can have natural feelings of love and affection toward others, like our parents, children, etc. However, the love of Allah must supersede all relationships.

HUMILITY ▸ We may be good at certain things in this world. We must recognize and acknowledge always that Allah is the greatest and we are nothing in front of Him.

3. ACTIONS OF THE TONGUE

Only *du'aa* for Allah. Only *Adhkaar* (remembrance) that reminds us of Allah. No *du'aa* to the dead, pious people, or to Jinns.

4. PHYSICAL ACTIONS

No bowing, prostrating, feeling or sacrificing dedicated to anyone other than Allah.

5. FINANCIAL ACTIONS

Sadaqah and *Zakah* are only for Allah. No sacrificing to the pious or deceased; no sadaqah at graves or so-called sacred places.

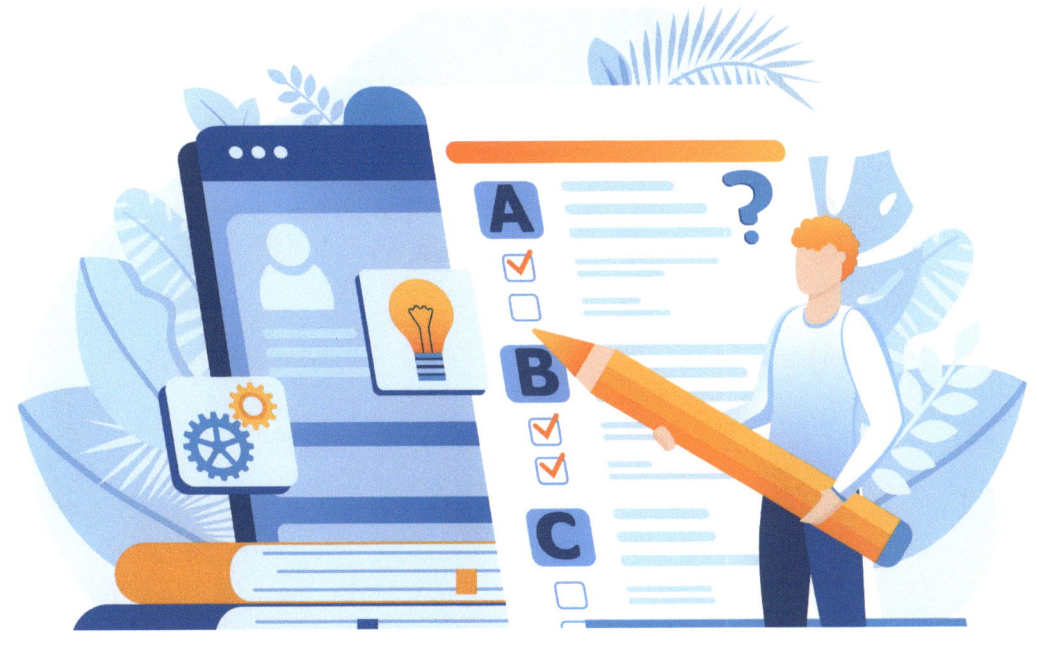

CHAPTER 11

REVIEW AND REFLECT QUESTIONS

1

Some Muslims celebrate the birthday of the Prophet *sallAllahu 'alayhi wa sallam* and they say it is out of their sincere love for him *sallAllahu 'alayhi wa sallam*. Their intentions may be sincere, but there is a mistake in their actions. Using what you learned in this chapter, what mistake is being made?

2

Allah says in the Qur'an, *"Have you seen he who has taken as his god his [own] desire."* (Al-Jaathiyah [45:23]) How does someone's desires become their god?

3

Jamila hears you saying that you are having a problem. She tells you she knows a really pious person and she'll ask her to pray for you. From what you learned in this chapter, what would your response be to Jamila?

www.ingramcontent.com/pod-product-compliance
Lightning Source LLC
Chambersburg PA
CBHW041544220426
43665CB00002B/33